Rehearsing for Doomsday

Rehearsing for Doomsday

Memoir of a Nuclear Missile Crew Commander

Scott Cook

McFarland & Company, Inc., Publishers
Jefferson, North Carolina

ISBN (print) 978-1-4766-8637-0
ISBN (ebook) 978-1-4766-4493-6

LIBRARY OF CONGRESS AND BRITISH LIBRARY
CATALOGUING DATA ARE AVAILABLE

Library of Congress Control Number 2021043142

Front cover: New missileers at Grand Forks Air Force Base;
On the left is Mitch Catanzaro, the author's roommate at
officer training, the author is at right (courtesy Mitch Catanzaro);
background: Minuteman launching from Vandenberg
with mountains in background (Air Force photograph)

Printed in the United States of America

*McFarland & Company, Inc., Publishers
Box 611, Jefferson, North Carolina 28640
www.mcfarlandpub.com*

Dedicated to my mother,
who introduced me to the wonderful world of books,
gave me the encouragement to write one, and
most importantly, taught me to love God's Book.

Table of Contents

Preface

This is a personal story, not an academic volume. It wasn't written as either a defense of, or repudiation of nuclear weapons. They exist. And, right or wrong, the United States government has made a series of decisions based on that reality.

This book is also not a critique of national policy, military strategy or a deep dive into the moral questions surrounding nuclear weapons. These are all important topics and I have my personal opinions. But I'm no expert. There are library shelves full of other works which address those subjects much better than I ever could.

This is the story of a young boarding school physical education teacher who found himself on the front lines of nuclear deterrence. That's the one topic about which I can proudly say, "I am an expert."

I tried to relate my experiences in a way that was accessible to the average reader, who may not know a reentry vehicle from a recreational vehicle. Therefore, military jargon and technical descriptions, while not totally expunged, have been greatly minimized. For instance, you will not be subjected to endless pages describing the detailed inner workings of the Minuteman III missile's inertial guidance system. And for that you should give thanks.

The story of the U.S. Air Force missileer is an important one. After the nuclear scientists have created, the national policy makers have decided, and the president and generals have commanded, the ultimate burden to launch a nuclear weapon falls to a small group of junior officers, geographically isolated in two-person crews.

As you might imagine, missile duty was not a sought-after assignment by most. In my era, there were many more "volun-told" crew members than volunteers. Yet, once a military officer takes the oath of office, he or she is essentially agreeing to whatever Uncle Sam assigns them.

Of course, I can't discuss every aspect of my missileer experience. Much of those duties involved classified information, which for security reasons must still be protected.

Also, I have employed pseudonyms for almost everyone mentioned. The few exceptions are my family members, a couple of close friends and a few public figures. The other friends and colleagues aren't public figures and may not want to be identified.

A word about North Dakota: I apologize up front for the jokes and less-than-flattering remarks about this great state. I have nothing personal against North Dakota or its people and I believe North Dakotans are some of the most hard-working, resilient and good-hearted folks in this country. If the missile fields were in rural Oklahoma or Iowa, those states would probably receive the same treatment.

But I *was* stationed in North Dakota and there's no getting around it— the Grand Forks area is a bleak, isolated and frigid stretch of land. Young officers, already stuck in an unwanted career field, channeled much of their frustration into complaining about their environment. That is common.

Grand Forks could be a lonely assignment because not many family members or friends ventured that far north to visit. Moreover, the local populace, although not unfriendly, could be somewhat stand-offish towards the military members living in their community. To be fair, maybe it was asking too much for North Dakotans to be enthused about the Air Force planting hundreds of nuclear missiles in their backyard.

I need to thank a few people. First, much gratitude goes to my parents and my brother, Todd, who read every word I wrote and gave me invaluable feedback. This book would not exist without their support, advice and encouragement. Thanks also to my beautiful wife, Beth, and our four children, Brett, Ben, Tori and Lindsay. I never cared much about where I was assigned as long as they were with me. They were and are my living, breathing therapy. And most of all, praise to God from whom all blessings flow. He has sustained me and walked beside me all these years.

CHAPTER 1

How Did I Get Here?

Full disclosure: There isn't any button. You don't launch a Minuteman III intercontinental ballistic missile (ICBM) tipped with a 150 kiloton nuclear warhead with the push of a button. You insert a key into a console and turn it. At least, that's how we were trained in 1989 when I was first assigned to missile crew duty. It was like starting a car, except with a million more horses under the hood. And no brakes. Once that beast goes, there's no stopping it.

Thankfully, I never had to "turn keys" for real. But my crew partner and I practiced World War III every month in the simulator on base. Then I'd drive home and read a bedtime story to my kids. Not your typical job.

In our extensive Air Force training we learned that simply turning our keys wouldn't launch a bottle rocket, much less an ICBM. First, we needed to input the correct launch codes. Those codes were secured hundreds of miles away, their release authorized by only one man. The guy living at 1600 Pennsylvania Avenue in Washington, D.C.

Yet even with the codes, two crew partners simultaneously turning keys equaled just one launch vote. You needed two votes to launch an ICBM. The other vote came from a second launch crew in another capsule. ICBM math is 4+2 = 1. Four crew members plus their two launch votes equal one launch.

So, despite what you might have read in a techno-thriller or seen in a movie, no one accidentally hits a button and launches a nuke. Nor is a deranged missile launch officer, or a group of them, able to deliberately launch an ICBM without authorization. There are too many safeguards, most of which are classified.

One of the few pleasant surprises during my crew duty in North Dakota was learning how secure nuclear launch systems really are. One of the many unpleasant surprises was learning how long North Dakota winters are. Spring, summer and fall were just weeks impersonating seasons. Great people up north. Rough environment.

When it's minus 20 degrees outside and you're pulling the graveyard

3

shift in a steel capsule buried 60 feet below the frozen tundra, you have ample time for personal reflection. Too much time. Depressing questions gnaw at your brain. Questions like "How did I end up here?" Or, "Why didn't I talk to that Navy recruiter instead?"

Like most kids, I wanted to be an astronaut or a major league baseball player when I grew up. Never did I dream of one day lobbing ten nuclear missiles over the North Pole, raining death and destruction on some unseen country.

I wasn't alone. When I began missile crew duty in the fall of 1989, there were several hundred crew members manning consoles in Montana, South Dakota, Missouri, Wyoming, and two North Dakota locations. These crews in their buried launch control centers monitored hundreds of missiles housed in nearby silos.

Like me, few crew members had chosen this profession. We wanted to become Air Force officers and four years on missile crew was the price of admission. So, we all took our place in a long line of subterranean sentinels that first formed in 1959. Since that year, there hasn't been a single moment when missile launch crews have not been on alert, ready to defend our country against a nuclear attack.

I'm proud that the Russians never attacked us during any of my 246 alert shifts. I guess they didn't want to mess with Lieutenant Cook. You're welcome, America.

I'm not a violent person. I've never thrown a punch in anger my entire life. My weapons experience consists of firing a handgun three times—all at ranges during required Air Force training. So, back to my graveyard shift question. How did a nice guy like me end up with his finger on the trigger of the most devastating weapon in human history? How does anyone? For me, that answer began a thousand miles and two years removed from the first day I set foot in an Air Force launch control center.

CHAPTER 2

Those Who Can't Teach...

I don't recall why I kicked Carson out of class that afternoon. I do remember what happened next. After reciting his many transgressions, I told him to stay by the door until the bell rang. Carson spat back, "I ain't standing out here!" and began to walk off. I grabbed his arm. He jerked away and strode towards the school building exit.

Using my best command voice, I called after him, "Get back here now or you're in real trouble." He paused at the exit, a safe distance away, and told me to go perform a sexual act on myself. Then, a final volley. "If you ever touch me again, I'll wipe the floor with you!" And Carson wasn't even one of my problem kids.

His threat would have been comical if it weren't so sad. We both knew that once I reported this, our vice principal would do much more than touch Carson. It would likely be an up close and personal session the young man wouldn't forget. They didn't mess around at boarding school. As Carson stormed out of the building, one truth crystalized for me: I had chosen the wrong profession.

A move in one direction is typically a rejection of another. My march towards the military began as a young, disillusioned teacher at a Baptist boarding school in southern Virginia. "Disillusioned" probably describes half of the teaching profession, but boarding school is a unique challenge. The students are the school's responsibility 24 hours a day, seven days a week. At our school, teachers like my wife and I were required to supervise student meals, after-hour activities, weekend events and even act as chaperones in church on Sundays.

Thankfully, my coworkers were very supportive. Our teacher's lounge served as foxhole, safe space, group therapy session and stand-up comedy club. We bonded like a combat unit under siege. Our students could be a tough lot.

Oak Hill Academy advertised itself as a place which turned wayward youth back to the road of success. For the most part, that was true. The school's motto is "There's no such thing as underachieving students, only unmotivated ones."

Whatever the label, the majority of our 150 students fell into one of two categories: passively disengaged or actively rebellious. Exasperated parents had deposited most of them on our doorstep, hoping we could perform miracles.

So, every fall they arrived. Sullen long-haired boys wearing black Led Zeppelin t-shirts. Pouty girls with heavy black eyeliner, dressed like Goth versions of Madonna.

Despite the varied fashion choices, most came with the same accessory—attitude. A commodity which they generously shared with the faculty and staff. For novice teachers like us, it was time to buckle our seat belts and return the tray table to the upright position. There was turbulence ahead.

Most parents understood the challenge they were handing us. If we couldn't make any progress academically, at least their son or daughter would be separated from the bad influences back home.

If separation was the goal, Oak Hill Academy was your place. Founded in 1878 and nestled in the foothills of southwest Virginia, the school was only a mile up the road from Mouth of Wilson, a "town" that should have been sued for false advertising. It was actually a huddle of drab buildings gathered around one stoplight near a bend in the Wilson River. The business district consisted of a general store, a tiny post office and a gas station that also doubled as a Ford dealership.

Every year students tried to run away. They'd sneak down to the main road and stick out their thumb to hitchhike. Invariably a kind farmer in a battered pick-up would stop and tell them to hop in. Then, he'd drive them back up the hill to the school Administration building, waving a friendly good-bye to the principal before rumbling back down the road.

The isolation was pervasive, especially for teachers like us who lived on-campus. The nearest grocery store was the Piggly Wiggly in Independence, 14 miles of winding road away. Cable television? Sorry. The cable didn't reach that far. To change channels on our home television I had to scale the roof and hand-turn the antenna until Beth yelled, "Stop! Stop! That's good!"

Our isolation was even more pronounced during the summer months, when school was out and the buildings sat dark and empty. In the evening, you could sit on your front porch and actually hear the silence. Late at night we knew other teachers were home in bed because we could hear them snoring. It was either peaceful or deeply disturbing, depending on your mood.

However, the students had it tougher. Their school days were scheduled from sunup to lights out with classes, evening study halls, dorm chores and little free time. They could only make one phone call a week and weren't allowed to have a car. I felt sorry for them.

Sensitive to the fact that too much unsupervised time led to trouble, especially on weekends, the administration worked hard to keep the students occupied and entertained. There were dances, movies in the gym, organized clubs and a variety of intramural sports. During good weather they transported the kids off campus for picnics, hiking and canoeing on the nearby river. On one river outing, a homesick boy refused to get out of the van. He sat there for two hours staring at a photo of his girlfriend back home.

One major challenge was keeping the sexes apart after hours. With numerous buildings, trees, bushes, barns and other hiding places, that wasn't easy. Couples in various stages of intertwinement were discovered in unlocked school vans, under bleachers and even in the reference section of the school library. Coats and blankets had to be banned from movie night because of the activity they were hiding underneath—it wasn't sharing popcorn.

Belligerent attitudes were another challenge. In this area, the school took a hard stance. Threatening the staff or bullying other students was not tolerated. The school had no security office and the nearest police station was miles away. Thus, the on-campus staff had to ensure the safety of all 200 people. There were holes in certain office walls that were rumored to be caused either by a student's body being shoved against them or a staff member's fist, used as a visual motivator. True or not, the rumors themselves were a behavioral deterrent.

Our principal, Mr. Prescott, was the chief enforcer. A burly bear of a man, he had a persona which inspired both affection and fear—a blend of ordained minister, southern gentleman, and Hulk Hogan. The kids loved him but knew he was not to be trifled with.

One minute he'd be out front of the school graciously greeting the students on their way to class. "Why, Miss Jones, that's a lovely book bag you have there! Move along now, gentlemen. That ole bell's gonna catch you." The next moment, the Hulk might be unleashed. Like a sonic boom, his voice would echo from the administration building as he welcomed a troublemaker into his office. "Get in here, boy! Time to open up those ears and close that mouth or I'll assist you in both!" Whoever that unlucky kid was, he inevitably emerged minutes later a more contrite, contributing member of society.

Despite the challenges, Oak Hill was an excellent school with a core of good kids just trying to get along. The teachers were dedicated and, for the most part, gave the students much needed attention and praise. It was rewarding to see the troubled ones begin to flourish as the school year progressed. Most raised their grades and left us as much more pleasant and motivated young people than when they arrived.

Ironically, our punishment for turning students around was having their parents immediately take them back. We were happy for the kids, but wished we had more time to enjoy the fruits of our labor.

And many days it *was* labor. I admired my fellow teachers who didn't allow the kids' bad attitudes to faze them. They knew that much of the defiant bravado was a cloak to hide deep insecurities. I knew this too, but still found it hard not to resent the disrespectful behavior. Many days I returned home, stomach churning due to some student's antics. I wasn't at Oak Hill long before I began to question whether I was cut out for this line of work.

I taught Psychology and General Math but my primary subject was the one in which I had obtained my degree—Physical Education (P.E.). In retrospect, this degree had not been a wise choice. Like many college kids, I picked a major based on my personal interests rather than whether or not it would lead to a fulfilling career.

Most P.E. majors have a chip on their shoulders. They know society does not hold their subject matter in high regard. My college P.E. professors would cringe whenever they heard someone refer to "gym class." "It's *physical education*," Dr. Harvey would huff. "A gym is a place, not a subject!"

Yet, at Oak Hill the students, and even the administration, had trouble connecting the word "education" with my subject. Their experience had been with P.E. teachers like the pot-bellied football coach who stands on the sidelines twirling a whistle and flirting with giggly girls who never seem to dress out.

I was determined to be different. I would educate my students in aerobic fitness concepts, measure individual progress in strength and flexibility tests, teach little-known sports skills like the proper tennis racket grip for the back hand. I would be cool. I would be respected. I would be hit with reality.

Like many before me, I underestimated the determined apathy of the average high school student. I was also disappointed to learn that my class was graded Pass/Fail. So much for measuring achievement. To add further frustration, Oak Hill didn't have any substitute teachers. If a teacher called in sick, their classes were sent to the gym. On those days I was forced to cancel my own classes and watch the missing teacher's students. I began to feel that I was wasting my God-given potential. I was on the dean's list throughout college and hadn't spent four years of private school tuition to become a glorified recess supervisor.

The administration tried to be supportive, in their own way. Vice principal: "Coach, everybody dressing out in your class? Jennifer Adams tried to get me to sign off another excuse note, but I told her that I did take Biology in school and there's no way she can have two periods in three weeks. And how 'bout Joey Johnson? Is that boy flying straight? If he gives you trouble, send him my way and we'll have a come-to-Jesus meeting, all right?" They were great colleagues but I was not the right guy for this type of work.

I was at Oak Hill primarily for one reason. My wife's cousin, Steve Smith, was the new head basketball coach and asked me to be his assistant. This wasn't just a job. It was a once-in-a-lifetime coaching opportunity. The basketball program at Oak Hill was the best in the country.

The story of how a small Baptist boarding school became a basketball powerhouse deserves its own book. The short version is that in the late 1970s, the school's president approved a crazy plan presented by his son, also the varsity basketball coach. He asked to travel to New York City and recruit three or four elite basketball players to come to Oak Hill for their senior year. His sales pitch was that the school's remote location and strong academics would help them get the grades they needed to qualify for a Division I college basketball scholarship. Also, Oak Hill would offer them free tuition, including room and board.

It would be a mutually beneficial arrangement. Oak Hill would gain free publicity by fielding a top national high school basketball team and the players would gain the academic help and focused environment that was hard to come by in the city.

Unbelievably, the plan worked. The school started beating the sneakers off every school in Virginia and at the end of the year, some of the players who had enrolled with shaky grades raised their averages enough to earn college scholarships. The news spread and the program began to gain momentum.

By 1985, the president's son had moved on and the school had hired Steve, the former assistant, as the new head coach. That created an opening for an assistant coach. Both Steve and I attended Asbury College, a small Christian liberal arts school in Kentucky. He was several years ahead of me, but we had frequently crossed paths on the pick-up basketball court. More importantly, I had married his beautiful, raven-haired cousin, Beth Smith. She was a teacher also, so we were a two-for-one deal.

By the time we arrived, Steve didn't need to go out and recruit players. He simply answered the phone as the parents, mentors and interested college coaches of potential players advocated for a spot on the team. During my tenure, it wasn't unusual to not meet a player until he arrived on campus for the first day of school. In some instances, we had never even seen a picture of the kid.

There were issues assimilating black teenagers from the inner-city into a predominantly white upper-class student body in rural Virginia.

Many of our players were terribly homesick and almost every year a couple were sent home because of various misbehavior problems. My first year, we had a player, just a junior, but already a New York City playground legend. One recruiter compared him to an NBA superstar by dubbing him "Magic Johnson with a better jump shot." We soon learned that this young man, although a good-hearted person, was actually "Magic Johnson with a minor drug problem." He only lasted a couple months.

Most of our players, though, persevered and were fun to be around. They worked on their academics and reluctantly submitted to, what were often, stringent school rules. They knew this might be their last chance to bolster their grades and earn a college scholarship.

My three years of coaching were a basketball junkie's heaven. Our first season we were 25–1 and ranked fourth in the country by *USA Today*. Our star player was a McDonald's All-American. He is still the most ferocious high school dunker I've ever seen. One high school scout described him as "Evel Knievel without the motorcycle." We also had a 7'3" center from Argentina who spoke almost no English when he arrived. All of our bench players earned college scholarships that year.

Unbelievably, the previous season I had been coaching pimple-faced ninth graders at a junior high school in Nicholasville, Kentucky. It was like driving a Ford Escort and suddenly being handed the keys to a Ferrari.

Our second year the team was just as good, with an identical record, losing our first game, but then winning 25 in a row. We had two more All-Americans. One went on to college and led the Big East conference in scoring. The other later played for the Indiana Pacers. The former, a 6'7" bull of a kid, broke several Oak Hill scoring records along with three opponents' noses—accidently, of course.

Great high school talent attracts great interest from college coaches and the media. It wasn't uncommon during practice to glance over at the bleachers and see Jim Valvano from North Carolina State or Jim Boeheim, head coach at Syracuse University, watching our team, along with a half-dozen other college assistants. After one game in Philadelphia, a young charismatic assistant coach from the University of Pittsburgh tagged along with us to eat at McDonalds. I never dreamed that John Calipari would one day coach my beloved University of Kentucky Wildcats.

That year, *Sports Illustrated* sent a writer and photographer to trail us for a week as background for a feature story. The Hall of Fame sportswriter, Bob Ryan, also stopped by and regaled us with stories about Larry Bird. It was all very surreal. I'd done nothing to deserve such a position other than my relationship with Steve.

The travel wasn't bad either. Because few teams wanted to drive to Mouth of Wilson to get beat by 30 points, we played in a lot of tournaments throughout the east coast and father away. Many of those tournaments paid our travel expenses to participate and improve their attendance. We played two Christmas tournaments in Las Vegas, a series of games in the Virgin Islands and others in New York City, Philadelphia, Cincinnati, and Washington, D.C. Today, top high school teams travel across the country for high-profile tournaments. But in 1986 we were an oddity.

My initial plan was to leverage my Oak Hill experience to eventually move on and coach in the college ranks. However, after an up-close look at the recruiting game, I changed my mind. Junior assistants were more traveling salesmen than coaches, primarily relied upon to cajole high school superstars to sign with their college. Even if you recruited top talent, the entire staff could be fired at will, due to a losing season. I wanted more stability in my life.

Steve intended to make his Oak Hill stay a short one, also. We both joked as other teachers received their ten-year plaques at graduation ceremonies. Not us. Oak Hill got the last laugh though, at least in Steve's case. He is still there, more than 30 years after I left. Not that the compensation hasn't been sweet. As of this writing, Steve has over 1,100 career wins, the third most of any high school basketball coach in history. Also, his teams have won several national championships. Twenty-nine of his former players were eventually drafted by the NBA, including stars like Carmelo Anthony and Kevin Durant. I expect he'll eventually be inducted into the Naismith Basketball Hall of Fame. Not bad for a guy who, like me, attended a small college that didn't even field an intercollegiate basketball team.

Yet as wonderful as it was, even the pinnacle of high school basketball didn't outweigh my unhappiness with teaching and the school's geographic isolation. I was determined to make a change.

CHAPTER 3

Choose Your Service

Although I'd never envisioned myself wearing a uniform outside of the baseball variety, the growing appeal of a military career seemed natural. I was the son of a career military officer. My father had recently retired after 22 years as a Navy chaplain. Those years included two tours in Vietnam, counseling cheating spouses, comforting wounded Marines, making family death notifications and holding weekly services, while also dealing with the rough-and-tumble world of everyday military life. While my father responded to the personal crises of others each day, I was blissfully playing Little League baseball and enduring *tough* living conditions in places like San Diego, California, and Pearl City, Hawaii.

Like all military families, we had to uproot every few years. But that seemed normal. I pitied the kids who were sentenced to 18 years in the same boring town. To me, each move was an adventure. Who wouldn't want to take a ship to Hawaii and then live there for three years? Or drive from California to a new home in Tennessee? Granted, leaving friends wasn't easy, but my best ones—my brothers—always came along. It was an educational and exciting life. In 1988, that's what I wanted for Beth and our young son, Brett. Not 10 more years of driving 35 miles to Galax for a K-Mart shopping spree.

Beyond a richer family life, I dreamed of a job with more mutual respect, discipline, variety and opportunity for advancement. The military seemed to check all those boxes. It was an honorable profession. It also might be nice to be saluted and called "sir" instead of dealing with sullen teens who threaten to wipe the floor with you. But if I had to boil it down to one driving motivation, it was for greater respect. From society and from my peers.

Don't misunderstand me. Teaching is a wonderful and vital profession. But like the military, it's not for everyone. The people who sign up for it are never paid enough money or appreciation. Almost anyone can stand up in front of a class and give a lesson. But to discipline without degrading? To inspire and motivate? To simultaneously connect with and focus 30 different personalities? That's a gift and few have it. I wasn't sure that I did.

But I needed the support of my wife for such a radical change. I wanted her to embrace this adventure as my mother had. Luckily, in Beth Cook I had a ringer. Like me, she was a military brat. The daughter of an Air Force chaplain, she had grown up in such exotic places as Okinawa, Pakistan and 1960s Southern California. Becoming a military wife would be like going home for her. That was critical. As I learned from my dad's chaplain experience counseling young couples, many a military marriage fails because the spouse never acclimates to the separation and frequent moves.

When we first met in college, Beth and I discovered we were among of the few students from military families. I was sure it was a sign we were meant to be together. I was looking hard for signs because she was beautiful. Still is.

As a young husband, I wanted to make her proud of my judgment. Yet, some of my early decisions in our marriage had not been the best. Only a month into wedded bliss, I depleted a good chunk of our meager savings to buy a used color television. When I drove over to the seller's home to take a look, the picture was fuzzy. The owner assured me that it was because their trailer sat in a low valley that didn't get good reception.

To my wife's great disappointment, $300 later, the television demonstrated its versatility by providing the same fuzzy reception in our third-floor apartment. An apartment which had all the charm of a Dickens-novel sweatshop. The view out our cracked living room window was a dirty brick wall. This low-rent love nest was another of my choices—to save money of course. To save money so we could blow it on a television that made every show appear to be taking place in a blizzard.

But my most infamous first-year decision was made the day I came home and declared that I had a big trade in the works.

"Hon, I met this young lady who has a gently used Ford Granada she's selling."

Beth smiled indulgently. "Scott, we don't have enough money to buy another car." She stared over at our color television in case I didn't get her meaning.

"Yeah, I know. I know. But I asked her and she would be willing to make a straight-up trade for another car, like, well, our Fiat."

Raised eyebrows and no smile. "You mean *my* Fiat? The one my dad bought me?"

"Well, it's really *our* Fiat since we're married now, right?" *Silence.* "Right?"

"Scott, I love the Fiat. It's sporty and I like driving a stick."

"Yeah, but it's not very practical. We really need a bigger car to haul groceries and our kids when we…"

"Excuse me?"

"Well, we'll have kids eventually. And when we do, we can't drive them around in a tiny sports car. It's just not safe."

I kept up my pitch but soon realized that Beth would rather trade me than the Fiat. After a week, I finally wore her down and we made the trade. The Granada was a beautiful big car. And it ran great. For five months. Before it broke down and cost $1200 to fix. It was only worth $1800 at the time.

So, my decision-making track record was a bit spotty. But by our third year at Oak Hill, even Beth knew that boarding-school life was not a long-term situation for us. We needed a change.

If I was going to take that big step, I first had to decide which branch of service to apply for. I would love to tell you I made this critical decision based on exhaustive research. I would be lying.

The Navy was crossed off my list for two reasons. First, I didn't want to be at sea all the time and away from my family. Second, my stomach and the sea have a turbulent history. When I was ten, my dad took me on a deep-sea fishing outing in Hawaii with some of his friends. It didn't go well. The boat was small, the seas rolled, and so did my insides. As marlin were heaved into the boat, I heaved the contents of my stomach over the side—three times. Never eat two baloney and mustard sandwiches before going deep-sea fishing. It was only one data point, but I concluded that six months at sea on a cramped Navy ship wouldn't work for me.

I admired the Marines. My father was stationed with the Marines twice and they were a disciplined, motivated and proud group. I had even graduated from the high school on Quantico Marine Corps Base in Virginia. Yet the leathernecks were a little too hardcore for my personality. I couldn't envision myself with a shaved head, spending my days knocking out hundreds of pull-ups and punctuating my sentences with "Oorah!"

I briefly considered the Army but they seemed to spend an unhealthy amount of time out in the mud and rain. I envisioned a career spent fighting foot fungus and accumulating skin rashes in places no one wants to scratch. And then there was the whole getting-shot-at deal.

Although I had no desire to be a pilot, the Air Force ultimately seemed the place for me. A kinder, gentler service: military lite. Unlike the other options, they believed in indoor plumbing, using their indoor voices, and an annual physical fitness test that didn't require Olympic-level training to pass.

Case in point: In 1992, the Air Force eliminated the annual 1.5-mile timed run and replaced it with an 8–15-minute heart-rate monitored stationary bicycle session. Now, that's my kind of people. This change was in response to an alarming number of hefty, two-pack-a-day-smoking chief master sergeants nearly having heart attacks trying to make their run times.

That wasn't my issue, but I was 10 years removed from my high school cross country experience. Any fitness test that involved the word "stationary" was okay by me.

So, the United States Air Force had won the lottery and would be offered my services. Where did I sign? Eagerness aside, one thing I did know was that officers weren't actually signed up like the enlisted recruits coming out of high school. An Air Force officer was competitively selected for commission. How that process worked, I wasn't sure. It was time to talk to a recruiter.

In the pre-internet days of 1988, I pulled out the dog-eared Jefferson County phone book and looked in the yellow pages under "Surrendering all Autonomy in Your Life." Not finding what I was looking for, I thumbed through the Rs and found the nearest Air Force recruiting office, located across the mountains in Bristol, Virginia. That Saturday morning, I set out down the road on a journey which would alter my life for the next three decades.

I parked on the street outside the small storefront office in the town's quaint little business district. It was a scene out of a World War II movie from the 1940s. The bell jingled as I entered. An eager young sergeant in a pressed blue uniform welcomed me with a vise-grip handshake. He offered me a seat opposite his desk, piled high with brochures, paperwork and a name plate bounded by small U.S. and Air Force flags.

I told him I was a college graduate, currently a teacher and interested in becoming an officer. That news seemed to throw him for a moment. He was clearly more accustomed to handling recent high school graduates wanting to enlist. Officer candidates were apparently about as rare as zebras in the greater Bristol area. I could read the disappointment on his face. All his memorized recruiting pitches would not apply to me. He was in uncharted waters and was forced to go to the manual, *How to Handle an Officer Candidate for Beginners.*

He nervously fished through a drawer before locating some reference material. We were both learning together. He informed me that there were three ways the Air Force selected officers. The first two didn't apply to me— the Air Force Academy in Colorado, and Reserve Officers' Training Corps (ROTC) units at various universities.

Whatever the Air Force needed beyond the graduates from these programs it generated through Officer Training School (OTS) in San Antonio, Texas. This was an intense three-month school, similar to the six-week Basic Military Training (BMT) that enlisted troops had to endure. If you made it through, you were commissioned as a second lieutenant in the Air Force and sent to your first assignment.

However, I was told, the application process to get accepted to OTS

was very competitive. It involved taking the Air Force Officer Qualification Test, obtaining strong recommendations, passing a physical and background check, writing an essay on why you wanted to be an officer, and
submitting a package (which also included your college transcripts) to a
selection board in Texas. The board would evaluate each package and select
a small group, possibly only 20 percent of the applicants, for a future OTS
class.

It dawned on me that I'd gotten the lottery analogy backwards. I was
the one who had to win the lottery. Apparently, the Air Force had plenty
of Scott Cooks out there who wanted to be officers. *Get in line, kid.* It was
humbling, to say the least.

Yet, I was determined to forge ahead. I took a folder crammed with
forms to be filled out, with deadlines highlighted in yellow. I thanked the
sergeant for his time and asked him to please not call the school. "No one
up there knows I'm doing this," I explained.

CHAPTER 4

Paper Underwear

The OTS application process was arduous. It was my first exposure to government paperwork and the bureaucracy that drives so many citizens crazy. Maybe, I thought, this is the first evaluation—the Air Force's way of weeding out the cowards early. If you couldn't handle the mental strain of hacking your way through their jungle of forms, then how could you survive a real enemy-infested jungle?

So, there were documents mailed, requests made, dozens of follow-up phone calls and multiple outings both back to Bristol to see my recruiter and to other locations, all of which I had to hide from friends and the school administration. No matter my reasons, I knew it would be awkward telling my Oak Hill family that I was looking to work elsewhere. Those were conversations I was determined to put off as long as I could. If I didn't get selected for OTS, I might never tell them.

On one trip to Bristol, my recruiter gave me yet another form which asked me to list my three preferences for Air Force jobs. *How considerate of them*, I thought. *They want me to be happy.* I filled out three choices, my number one being Intelligence Officer. I'd always enjoyed detective and spy stories. Intelligence gathering sounded interesting.

When I returned the completed form to my recruiter, he read my choices with a frown. "You know," he said gently, "what they really need are missile launch officers."

"Missile launch officers?" I answered. Not the wittiest response, but he had thrown me. The form was asking for *my* preferences, right? And besides, how do those guys occupy themselves on days when there isn't a war going on? Do they wash and wax the missile?

"What do missile officers do?" I asked.

The sergeant leaned forward. "Well, they sit on alert in case we're attacked, ready to launch their missiles at Russia. It's a very important job, part of the strategic defense triad of ICBMs, bombers and submarines."

A dim light glowed in my brain. *Oh, those guys—down in the silo with the nukes.* If there was one thing even the casual observer of 1980s current events knew about, it was the Cold War nuclear stand-off between the United States and the Soviet Union.

I also recalled that those missile silos weren't located near any beaches. "Where are the bases?" I asked suspiciously. The good sergeant turned in his desk chair, stood and began to move his index finger up towards a huge map of the United States. The finger traveled up past the southern states and into the Midwest. And kept moving north. My eyes widened as he hit that part of the country where the states are all shaped like big brownie squares in a pan. The states that no one ever goes to on vacation.

Still the finger crept higher. Finally, it stopped. Sheesh, was he pointing to Canada? Close. North Dakota. *North Dakota?* Was that area of the country actually inhabited? A shiver raced up my spine. His finger also traced South Dakota, Montana, Wyoming, and the one tropical location— rural Missouri.

"No, no, no. That's all right. I think I'll stick with my three choices," I said.

He smiled politely. "Just so you know, if you list missile launch officer as one of your choices, you have a better shot at being selected for OTS. They really need missile launch officers."

"I know. You said that," I replied. "I think I'll stick with my list." As I drove off, I could see him looking out the window, slowly shaking his head.

One item on my to-do list was getting an Air Force physical. They wouldn't even consider my application package unless I was certified as physically fit to serve. No big deal. I taught P.E. for Pete's sake and was even jogging three miles a day.

Actually, three miles a night. In the dark. One night, I couldn't see the beginning of the administration building board walk too well, tripped and fell, slicing my knee open. Since it was late and the nearest emergency room was miles away, I slid the skin flap back up and wrapped it in a bandage. Stitches would have been a better choice. It healed but I still have an ugly scar on that knee today. Another swimwear modeling career ruined.

The Air Force physical did not involve any nighttime running so I was good. It took place at the nearest Military Entrance Processing Station (MEPS) in Beckley, West Virginia, an inconvenient two-hour drive away. Fortunately, my physical was scheduled for a Saturday, so I didn't need an excuse to miss work.

Each interaction with the Air Force provided a little more insight into my future employer. What I learned in Beckley was that the Air Force wasn't overly concerned with my modesty or personal privacy. I was herded into a small changing area with 15–20 other hopefuls, most much younger than me. We were told to strip down to our underwear.

One young fellow, who looked like he had possibly arrived from the mountains on horseback, informed the MEPS sergeant that he wasn't wearing underwear. The sergeant wasn't pleased with this bit of news. However, he immediately produced a pair of paper underwear, which the young man thankfully slipped on.

I wasn't sure what was more incredible to me: that a young man would show up to a formal Air Force physical without underwear—or that enough recruits were showing up without underwear that the MEPS station found it necessary to purchase paper substitutes. *No, son, we won't need that pair back. Consider it your gift from the United States government.*

Before I could ponder this too deeply, we were lined up and put through various pokings and proddings, culminating in the grand finale—a parade! We were ushered into a large room where a bored-looking doctor sat in the center, spilling over a small metal folding chair. Still in our underwear, we were told to walk quickly in a big circle around him for several minutes.

This seemed somewhat undignified to me, but I complied because, after all, he was a medical professional. It could only have been worse if they played circus music and gave us party hats and tiny flags to wave. I assume in this instance the doctor was evaluating our gait to ensure we could handle extended marches or long runs without injury. Or maybe he was just seeing if we would follow orders, no matter how ridiculous.

The interview portion consisted of intimate questions about our medical history, well within earshot of the other recruits. The medical personnel were certainly not using their library voices. "Now tell me again, how long have you had that enormous hairy wart on your backside?"

I was glad to pass the physical but even happier to get out of there. I drove away a relieved, fully-clothed man, my dignity temporarily restored.

Soon, my completed OTS application package was assembled and submitted by the recruiter. A couple months later, he called me. "Mr. Cook, I have some good news and bad news."

"All right," I responded cautiously. "What's the good news?"

"Congratulations. You've been selected for an OTS class beginning in June. You were one of only 60 selected by the board, out of 400 applicants."

I let out a whoop. "All right! Wow, what a relief. Thanks for all your help putting my package together. Now what's the bad news?"

"They selected you as a missile launch officer."

I was stunned. "What? How can that be? That wasn't one of my three choices. I thought I'd get one of those three or they wouldn't pick me at all. Can they do that?"

He laughed. "Sir, it's the U.S. government. They can do whatever they want. I know you didn't want missiles but when it comes down to it, they make their decisions based on the needs of the Air Force."

The needs of the Air Force. A truth that I would soon learn over and over again. My desires were secondary. Or thirdary. Whatever is well below "the needs of the Air Force."

I called my parents to let them know. I asked my dad if I should turn down the selection and re-apply, hoping to be selected for another job besides missiles. I'm glad we were talking by phone so I couldn't see his eyes roll.

"No," he replied evenly. "That's not how this works. If you turn it down, they won't ever consider you again. They want people who are willing to serve their country, whenever and wherever. If you don't like missiles, just do your best during that first assignment, then hopefully you'll have an opportunity to cross-train into another career field later." As usual, he was right.

It was now time to let Oak Hill Academy know my plans. Since it was already spring, I felt it was only right to resign quickly so they could hire my replacement. The school president was very understanding and said he was proud I had decided to serve. What a relief. Within a few weeks he had hired my replacement. Life was good.

A month later, I received another phone call from my recruiter. He said, "Sir, I have good news and bad news."

"What's the good news?" I asked, sensing a dark foreboding.

"The good news is that you have more time to be with your family *and* prepare for OTS!"

"What are you talking about?" I asked.

"Well, unfortunately that's the bad news," he replied. He continued, speaking about congressional budget cuts which were forcing the Air Force to reduce the number of OTS classes this fiscal year, etc. The bottom line was that my OTS class for that summer had been canceled. The next opportunity to go would be in another year, the summer of 1989.

"Can they do that?" I asked incredulously.

"They can do anything they want. It's the U.S. government."

This conversation seemed familiar. "But I just quit my job!" I wailed into the receiver. He was sympathetic but what could he do? I hung up in a trance. Beginning in July, I wouldn't have any more income from Oak Hill. I was counting on my Air Force pay to kick in then. Now I'd have a 12-month gap with no pay. Thankfully, Beth was still employed by the school.

I went to see the president again and shared my tale of woe. God bless him, he was very understanding—again. Right on the spot he created a new part-time position for me—study hall monitor. I would supervise four of those sessions every morning the following year and receive half my current pay. I thanked him profusely. Money would be tight, but we could make it for a year.

That fall, I began my demanding part-time job of study hall supervision. It was wonderful and gave me time to read Air Force history, to memorize the names, silhouettes and capabilities of Air Force aircraft and missiles as well as become more familiar with the nuclear deterrence mission. Then, only a month into the fall semester I received a call from my recruiter. Uh oh.

"What's the bad news?" I asked right away.

"Only good news," he said brightly. "Some additional funding has been found and now you'll begin OTS in November, the day after Thanksgiving."

"That's less than two months away," I said. I almost followed up with a "Can they do that?" but I was much smarter now.

Again, I went to my president and again, he was understanding and released me. How he was going to replace me in the middle of the school year, I didn't know. I felt bad but was grateful for patriots like him who were willing to help a young teacher follow his dream. I thanked him for *his* service.

I don't regret the years I spent at Oak Hill. Despite the frustrations, it was one of the most interesting periods of my life. Beth and I were blessed to meet some great kids, several of whom we still keep in contact with. Our coworkers were a fun group and Steve and his wife, Lisa, did all they could to make us feel at home. Yet after almost four years there, I knew it was time to go.

CHAPTER 5

What Kind of School Is This?

I arrived in San Antonio, Texas, with clean, cotton underwear (no paper ones for me) and some misconceptions about Officer Training School. The OTS guidebook, which I'd devoured cover to cover, had been slightly misleading. From its pictures and descriptions, I envisioned a 12-week experience similar to college, with a little housekeeping and marching thrown in. Turns out, it was the reverse.

During the day we attended academic classes and physical fitness sessions, coupled with the occasional small arms training or field exercise. However, most of our evenings and weekends were spent performing such vital combat skills as dusting, sweeping, mopping, ironing, buffing, scrubbing, marching, and the highly critical removal of excess uniform lint. In addition, we were ever vigilant in our goal to ensure that no personal item in our room was ever touched once it was put in place.

OTS had a place for everything. All clothes hangers had to be hung exactly two inches apart. Every item hung up had to have all buttons buttoned. All t-shirts, socks and underwear stowed in drawers were required to be folded in a precise way and placed in an exact location in said drawer. If said drawer was opened by the flight commander and an item shifted from its assigned spot—that was very bad. Demerits would be assigned. We weren't even allowed to have trash in our trash cans. When I graduated, I was more qualified to lead a flight of housekeeping staff into a dirty hotel room than a group of airmen into battle.

"Relax, Francis," one might say. *Demerits? Big deal!* Granted, OTS wasn't Navy SEAL training. However, excessive demerits could be a reason for program removal and, at the very least, could bed-post you—restrict you to base when your flight mates were allowed the rare free Saturday night in San Antonio.

The physical and academic demands of OTS were not so demanding. It was all mental. OTS was a thirteen-week mind game. Thirteen weeks, not twelve as the guidebook had said, because the first few days didn't count. They were pre-training days, whatever that meant.

From 5:00 a.m. until 10:30 p.m. we were kept busy performing tasks with insufficient time to finish them and insufficient understanding of why we were doing them. We came to realize that the mind-numbing, seemingly pointless rules were the Air Force's way to crank up the pressure. Would the trainees pull together, prioritize actions and perform under stress? Or would they get frustrated, angry and fall apart?

No matter how ridiculous the rules, we knew we had to follow them to graduate and get our coveted commission. No one wanted the humiliation of being sent home. I couldn't fathom facing the friends and family members who had just given me a rousing send-off. Most trainees who left, left early. One young lady in our flight quit on the third day. Another guy was quietly sent home after being found by his roommate sitting on his bed staring unresponsive into space. I wasn't happy, but I hadn't marched around a doctor in my underwear in West Virginia only to quit.

The day I arrived, there were approximately 350 officer trainees (OTs) in the program. A majority of them were tagged as future aircrew—pilots or navigators. I wasn't part of that group, probably because I had not scored well on the aeronautics portion of the qualification test. I imagine they had reviewed my test results and concluded that I had no business being in the vicinity of anything with wings. Remaining above ground might even be too risky. Underground was perfect. "Attention everyone. We have another candidate for missiles!"

OTS was divided into upper and lower classes. I was surprised to learn that the upper class, with only six weeks more experience under their belts, were responsible for supervising us lower class OTs in the quadrangle dorm area. Yet ultimately, the flight commanders were in charge. These junior Air Force officers were pulled from a variety of fields to spend a career-broadening assignment training us and evaluating our performance. A flight commander effectively had power over the life and death of the trainees in his or her white-gloved hands.

Flight commanders loved to inspect uniforms. We were required to keep six different uniform combinations accessible at all times. When told to change, we were given approximately 3–4 minutes to do so. Those frantic minutes were like backstage at the Miss Universe pageant between musical numbers, minus the flying sequined dresses or high heels. If I was wearing boots, 80 percent of my allotted changing time would be spent hopping around the room trying to pry my size thirteen monstrosities free from their leathery bonds.

Seventeen of us were assigned to Squadron 2, Flight 15—color blue. Our squadron name was "Cobra Two Strike Force." Slight hyperbole. Our main weapons turned out to be janitorial implements. Anywhere in the world that floors needed a good mopping and buffing, Cobra Two Strike Force was ready to deploy!

My roommate was Mitch Catanzaro, an easy-going yet laser-focused guy, about my age. He had already spent eight years in the Air Force as an imagery analyst. Mitch grew up in an Italian working-class family from Brooklyn, New York. He had enlisted in the Air Force right after high school. During his career, he worked his way up to the rank of technical sergeant and earned his bachelor's degree by taking evening and weekend classes. He was a sharp guy and his performance was impressive enough to win him this coveted slot at OTS.

I was glad to room with someone who had actually experienced the real Air Force. Mitch was happy to learn that my father was a former Navy chaplain. He thought it was lucky to room with the son of a priest. "The man upstairs will be looking out for us," he said with a grin. I explained that I wasn't Catholic, and my father wasn't a priest, but Mitch didn't care. In his mind, we had the heavenly hook-up. That theory would be tested.

I liked rooming with Mitch, but I was an introvert and missed the privacy of home. The only time you were truly alone at OTS was when you shut the door to the bathroom stall. *Heaven.* The first few weeks we weren't allowed off campus and were required to travel (i.e., march) everywhere as a flight of 17. This forced everyone to compromise to reach our objectives. I didn't realize it then, but these artificial pressures prepared me well for what I would soon face in my missile training.

Once we realized what we were up against as a flight, we put our heads together and shared ideas of how to meet these unending demands. We leaned heavily on the advice of prior enlisted guys like Mitch who had experienced most of this back in basic training. Some of these techniques, while effective, were not exactly approved by leadership. However, the flight commanders indulged some creativity, as long as it wasn't explicitly forbidden.

One example: We taped our underwear, t-shirts and socks to the bottom of the drawer so they wouldn't shift when the drawer was opened. Of course, once taped down you couldn't wear these items. Instead, they became our "museum piece," there for inspections only. The clean underwear, socks and t-shirts for wear were often stashed in a dirty laundry bag. Other items ended up hidden in the ceiling tiles. Although not approved for storage, these places were rarely inspected. Hidden items were dubbed "panicked" items and could earn a chunk of demerits if discovered.

To keep our beds perfect at all times we rarely slept in them. Mitch and I laid on top of the covers from time to time but almost never underneath. The one exception was "hotel night," the one night we could mess up the bedding because they would be stripped for laundry the next morning.

For several weeks when demerits were an issue, Mitch and I even slept on the linoleum floor of our room. We couldn't even use the pillows because they also had to stay pristine. So, my plastic briefcase became a very inadequate substitute. It was as uncomfortable as it sounds, but when you are on the move 18 hours a day, you can sleep almost anywhere.

Even 18 hours wasn't enough time to get everything done. The rule was lights out and in bed by 10:30 p.m. Many nights Mitch and I tip-toed about the dark room finishing our tasks. Sometimes upper classmen, who were allowed up a little later, would shine their flashlights under our door, catching our pattering feet. "Boy, looks like some big cockroaches scurrying around in there," they would loudly announce to each other.

We were up at 4:30 a.m., with chores done, out the dormitory door and formed up in our flight by 5:15. From there, it might be off to the athletic field for calisthenics under the stars or, even better, straight to breakfast.

Each day some poor soul was assigned the duty of flight leader. He or she would form us up into two columns and march us to the dining hall for meals, calling out commands. This short journey was fraught with danger because any small infraction noticed by a passing officer or upper classman could elicit one of the most dreaded commands in OTS—"Flight leader, halt your flight and report to me!"

Your flight was never halted so a passing officer could ask how your day was going or compliment you on the sharpness of your uniform. The offending flight leader was expected to halt the flight, then rush over and report to the officer.

"Sir, OT Twitchy reporting as ordered" (salutes).

"OT Twitchy, never drop your salute before a senior officer drops his."

"My apologies, sir" (salutes again, holding it until the officer finishes his salute).

"That's better, OT Twitchy. Now, you can write it (demerits) for improperly rendering customs and courtesies to a commissioned officer."

"Yes, sir."

"Now, OT Twitchy, the reason I stopped you was because one of the OTs in your flight is not holding his flashlight in the outside hand. As you know, all flashlights are to be held in the outside hand so their beam can properly illuminate any potential tripping hazards in the walkway ahead."

"Sir, I apologize for that oversight. I will correct it immediately."

"OT Twitchy, after you do that, please inform the offending OT that he can write it for a safety violation, as you can also as flight leader."

"Yes Sir." OT Twitchy salutes, does an about face and starts to stride back towards his flight.

"OT Twitchy! Did I excuse you to return to your flight?"

OT Twitchy scrambles back to the officer. "Sir, OT Twitchy requesting permission to return to my flight."

"Permission granted. You can also write it for not requesting permission to be dismissed. Have a great Air Force Day."

By the time OT Twitchy makes it back to his flight he is already a few demerits shy of being bed posted the following weekend. And it is just 5:35 a.m. on Monday morning!

The potential for such encounters made all flight leaders jittery in the pre-dawn trips to the dining hall. Many began seeing phantom officers everywhere and could be observed saluting small trees, large rocks, stray cats or basically anything that moved and might be wearing rank.

The shared destiny and misery of the flight created a strong bond. That was the intent. Beyond leadership, OTS strived to develop a sense of service before self and the ability to work as part of a team. The Air Force needed effective followers as well as effective leaders.

In the afternoons we played one of two sports—flickerball or one-pitch softball. As the name states, batters in one-pitch softball receive a single pitch, resulting in either a strike out, walk or the ball put in play. By itself, this rule speeds up the game considerably. Not enough, though, for our OTS instructors who constantly barked at players, "Move, move, move!" Players were often called out simply for not arriving at home plate fast enough to take their turn at bat. Even recreation became a stress test at officer training.

Flickerball was played outside between two goals. It was a convoluted cross between basketball and football with all the fun parts eliminated. Like one-pitch, flickerball was a twisted tangle of pointless rules and restrictions meant to eliminate any athletic advantage, create uncertainty and inject an endless number of penalties for infractions the infractor rarely understood. In other words, the perfect game for OTS.

The first few weekends we weren't allowed off base. Instead, we spent Friday nights mopping and buffing floors in the academic building. The building sat on a hill, so we could see the nearby highway and lights of the city beyond. Cars sped down the road taking groups of carefree people to clubs, restaurants and movies. High above, I could see the lighted signs beckoning customers towards shopping centers and restaurants. It looked like a neon paradise.

More than my freedom, I missed my wife and son. Some OTs, against the program's advice, had moved their wives and kids into local San Antonio apartments. OTs were only allowed off Medina Annex to see family members after the first three weeks, and even then, for only 24 hours from Saturday afternoon until Sunday afternoon. The rest of the week, family members were on their own, most in a strange city knowing no one. I would have loved even one day a week with my family but would have worried about them the other six. Beth was still working at Oak Hill, with all our friends and her mom there for support. I knew this was for the best.

So, I had to settle for rare weekend phone calls and letters. There was only one phone in the dorm and we had to get permission to use it—for official business only. Letters were my connection to Beth. Opening a letter from her was like opening an envelope of fresh mountain air. The affection and encouragement that flowed out put much-needed wind in my flagging sails. A reminder again of why I was doing this.

All the Friday night cleaning culminated in Saturday morning dorm inspections by our upper class. The Saturday morning inspection would be a comedy skit if it hadn't been treated so deadly serious. Squadrons were awarded points based on how they fared. These points were then added to others competitively earned during the week to crown an OTS squadron winner. Why anyone cared was beyond me. According to Mitch, none of these basic training awards meant spit to the real squadrons we were headed for after graduation.

Early Saturday morning, we were all required to form up outside our open dorm rooms, dressed in blues. Soon we were called to attention, eyes front, as the dreaded "train" hit our floor. The train was a single line of upper-class inspectors, marching almost nose to neck down the hall. At random spots they would be called to a halt and directed by the flight leader to inspect the room and two occupants either to the left or right. The performance of that room and occupants would greatly impact the squadron's inspection score. No pressure.

The worst location for your room was at either end of the hall. This was because the train was forced to stop at both locations. *As long as we're stopped, let's inspect these guys....* Guess where our room was? When the train picked a room, two of the inspectors would go inside and start examining it like a forensic crew at a crime scene. The two chaps outside would look over the two roommates' uniforms for violations and then give one of them a verbal quiz question. They then held up a card with four possible responses about six inches from the responder's nose. Without speaking, the OT would jerk his arm up and point to an answer. The questioner took note of the answer, re-formed the train and off they would go.

After the train had chugged down the stairs, everyone was ordered to go inside their rooms and lie quietly on their beds until summoned. OT nap time. Eventually, we would be roused and gathered in the lounge for the inspection results. If told we had finished second because someone left a sock in the laundry room dryer, there would be wailing and gnashing of teeth, lessons-learned committees formed, and emotional speeches made about "bringing our A games next week." Life in a training bubble can be surreal.

At times like these and in our academic lectures, Mitch was my reality check. He'd always lean over to whisper some version of this sentence:

"That's bull—." They don't do that in the real Air Force." I didn't know what the real Air Force was like, but apparently it didn't operate like OTS.

One of the most interesting exercises we did was the Leadership Reaction Course. The course consisted of 10 different outdoor stations. Each station was like a racquet ball court with no back wall. The 10-foot walls in the front and sides prevented us from seeing adjoining stations' set-up. Each station presented a war scenario problem that had to be solved within a specified time. It usually involved getting your group of five to six members with their simulated weapons and equipment through and over various obstacles.

To make the scenarios more difficult, restrictive rules were put in place. Certain areas were painted red to denote quicksand, land mines or other hazards. If stepped on, the red would "kill" team members or require everyone to halt while a precious minute ticked away. Traversing the obstacles was further complicated by rules preventing anyone who had successfully negotiated an obstacle from returning to help others.

Climbing over and around obstacles wasn't easy either. Sometimes your equipment was two boards, an eight-foot rope, a bucket and seven bricks. The objective was to figure out how to use those objects to get six people across a river and over a wall while carrying all your equipment.

Each scenario only required a small group, so the rest of us watched and helped the flight commander give constructive criticism afterwards. One person was designated the scenario leader and then evaluated on how he or she focused the group's efforts, divided up tasks based on strengths, maintained control over disagreeing factions and made timely decisions on when to reverse course when one idea was obviously not working. It was fun to watch, but not as fun to lead. This was especially true if your time expired with two of your flight members "dead" and the one heavy guy you couldn't get over the wall, still dangling by the rope.

By the time we made upper class at the program's mid-point, life began to change for the better. We knew the system now, were getting fewer demerits and no longer had an upper class to harass us. The pressure lessened and we began to feel more like potential officers.

As the final two weeks approached, a kind of siege mentality began to overcome the flight. No one wanted to make any last-minute mistakes which might result in expulsion or a slew of demerits. The easiest road to expulsion was an ethics violation so we meticulously avoided any perception of lying or cheating.

OTS introduced a new concept that aided us in this goal. It was called "popping off." The idea was that, although lying wasn't tolerated, if an OT was questioned and under stress blurted out an untruth, it was recoverable. The blurted lie could be excused as "popping off," a response that was technically a lie, but said without thinking. Upon realizing the mistake, if you immediately confessed, it was not held against you as an ethics violation. A lying mulligan as it were. However, if you didn't correct it and subsequently the lie was discovered, no apology could save you. You might just have popped off your Air Force career.

As graduation day approached, I realized that OTS had taught me three critical things that would stay with me forever: (1) attention to detail, (2) to think clearly under pressure and (3) to quickly prioritize actions in a time crunch. All of those were much more useful than anything I learned about aircraft, warfare, or Air Force customs and courtesies. All three tools would be vital in surviving the world of ICBMs and Strategic Air Command.

On March 17, 1989, our class graduated, culminating in a parade past the OTS leadership and cheering friends and family. Flight 2–15 never looked sharper in our uniforms. Mine fit better, helped by the 15 pounds I had lost during the 13 weeks. Beth, Brett, my parents and my Grandma Cook from Missouri were there to share that day with me.

After the parade, we were all commissioned in smaller ceremonies which took place in a large assembly hall. My father wore his Navy captain's uniform and administered the ceremonial oath to both myself and Mitch. We were now officially U.S. Air Force second lieutenants. Our wives slid new epaulets onto our shoulders with the single gold bars, "butter bars" as they are sometimes mockingly referred to. Yes, we were on the lowest rung of the officer ladder, but still felt like generals. A couple of sergeants came up and gave us our first salute. We gave them each a silver dollar—an Air Force tradition.

I've had happier days in my life. My wedding day and the births of my four children come to mind. But I've never had a prouder or more satisfying one.

CHAPTER 6

A Cold War Education

I confess. When I first learned I was headed for missile crew duty, I was somewhat ignorant about the political issues of nuclear weapons. I knew we had ICBMs, of course. You couldn't grow up in the 1970s and not know that the United States was in a Cold War stand-off with the Soviet Union. Freedom and democracy were being challenged by repressive regimes around the globe. On that side was the Soviet Union and then satellite states such as East Germany and Poland, as well as the oppressive governments of China and North Korea, and Cuba. Opposing them and their ideology stood the United States and their North Atlantic Treaty Organization (NATO) allies.

Both the United States and Russia were global powers, each with an arsenal of thousands of nuclear weapons targeting the other. Our missiles were distributed between three platforms: submarines ("boomers"), long-range bombers such as the B-52, and land-based ICBMs located in underground hardened silos. This distribution assured us that the Russians couldn't locate or accurately target all of our missiles in a conflict. Even so, the thought of nuclear war was deeply disturbing to most citizens.

Popular entertainment from the Cold War era exploited our anxiety. Many of the movie, book and television drama plots from my formative years revolved around the threat of a nuclear attack or the accidental launch of an ICBM. James Bond films used this scenario multiple times. Stanley Kubrick mined the concept for dark humor in his over-the-top classic *Dr. Strangelove or: How I Learned to Stop Worrying and Love the Bomb.*

Serious films like *Fail Safe* imagined more realistic scenarios where a bomber crew lost communications and mistakenly thought they had received the order to drop their nuclear weapons on Moscow. A made-for-television movie, *The Day After,* depicted the lead up to, and devastating aftermath of, a nuclear attack on the Unites States by Russia. The film showed cities leveled in the initial blast and fire engulfing millions of innocent people. Survivors were depicted after the blast emerging from bunkers only to choke on fall-out radiation and left to experience slow, agonizing deaths. It was pretty horrific stuff.

These fears were ratcheted up even more with the presidential election of Ronald Reagan in 1980. He had campaigned on taking a hard stance against Russia by building up the United States military and our missile defense. Critics saw this stance as provocative, pushing us closer to war instead of deterring one.

As my missile assignment loomed, I wanted to better understand my country's policies related to nuclear weapons and deterrence. There was no internet to *Google* this information, so I visited my 1988 alternative—the Grayson County Public Library.

By now, Reagan had been president for almost two full terms. There were plenty of books on nuclear armament and his role in the current debate. Since I hadn't read many political or policy books, I had the naïve belief that, like biographies or sport histories, these authors would be fairly even-handed in addressing this subject. Not so.

It seemed like almost every book I read was highly critical of the United States' nuclear weapons' policy. We had too many nuclear bombs, they agreed. We were also overly paranoid about the Soviet's capability. Mutually Assured Destruction (MAD) was a dangerous and ineffective theory for deterrence. Reagan was portrayed either as a dunce, senile, or a trigger-happy cowboy who was going to get us all killed.

I was taken aback. Where were the books defending the President and his administration's policies? There didn't seem to be any at the library. I concluded that fear sells more books than reassurance.

I was even more disappointed to see the military consistently portrayed in a negative light. In 1988, the depressing slog of the Vietnam War was still fresh in everyone's mind, soiling the military's reputation. Based on their view of the Vietnam War as a bungled, immoral endeavor, many in the media had little trust in the military's stewardship of something as powerful as nuclear weapons. Not very motivating for someone like me who was about to embark on an Air Force career in missiles.

Besides seeking an education in nuclear deterrence, I was also interested in the history, organization, and development of the current nuclear forces, especially our land-based ICBMs.

The early history seemed pretty straightforward. The U.S. was the first nation to develop a nuclear weapon and the only one to ever employ that capability. The atom bombs dropped on Hiroshima and Nagasaki in 1945 ended our war with Japan but began a nuclear arms race with others.

Following World War II, our former ally but now Cold War adversary, Russia, worked to reach parity with us in nuclear weapons. Our concern about their capability and what they might choose to do with it were further inflamed when Russia pushed past us in the space race. In 1957, when Russia launched the first successful satellite, Sputnik, Americans worried that an experimental satellite flying over the U.S. could lead to spy satellites, or even worse, a Russian bomb aimed at our cities. In reaction, we accelerated our ICBM program which we hoped would deter the Russians from any new aggression.

Gallons of ink have been spent writing about the wisdom, logic and motives behind the U.S. and Soviet build-up of new weapons. I'll leave that debate to minds much sharper than mine. Right or wrong, in the late 1950s, the United States began testing a long-range nuclear weapon capability.

I learned that the first ICBMs tested were the Atlas and Titan missiles. Versions of these would eventually be used in our early spaceflight program to propel astronauts such as John Glenn into low-earth orbit. Unfortunately, several of these early above-ground test launches demonstrated an unwanted tendency to blow themselves up, not in Russia, but right above their Cape Canaveral launch pads.

Early reliability and responsiveness were sadly lacking. For instance, the initial goal for this new ICBM system was to launch 25 percent of them within 15 minutes of orders and then another 25 percent up to two hours later. The assumption was that the other 50 percent would either fail or wouldn't be ready to launch at all. By the time I began my missile training, well over 90 percent of the nation's ICBM force were ready to launch at a moment's notice. An astounding improvement in only a couple decades.

The date of the first ICBM to be placed on launch alert was, ironically, Halloween, October 31, 1959. The Atlas D model was deployed at Vandenberg Air Force Base, above ground, inside what was referred to as a metal coffin. Each complex had three coffins and one control center. Upon orders, the missile was raised out of its coffin, fueled with propellant (a kerosene-based gas) and liquid oxygen, and launched. It was then led to its target by a radio inertial guidance system.

Eventually, the Atlas F model and Titan I missiles were housed in underground silos. Despite this extra protection and secrecy, there were still many issues to work through. The early missile systems were expensive, inaccurate and required an army of people to maintain them. For instance, on a typical day at a Titan I site there might be several dozen operators, security personnel, service troops and maintainers to keep three missiles up and running. Even when ordered to launch, the missiles had to be raised from their silo for several minutes beforehand, making them vulnerable at a most crucial time.

Because of these and other issues, in 1964–65 the Atlas I and Titan I were deactivated by the Secretary of Defense. Next in line was the improved Titan II ICBM, which carried a larger warhead and sat in the silo day to day, fully fueled and ready to be launched in minutes. Yet, it was still dangerous for the missile crew of two officers and two enlisted airmen to operate the missile from a control center separated from the fueled missile only by a short tunnel.

As the nation's ICBMs continued development, so did the crew members who were expected to be ready to launch these missiles 24 hours a day. Since there were sensitive nuclear-related components in these control centers, they were designated as "two-person concept" areas, meaning no one could be in the control center alone, or the only one awake inside. Yet, when pulling a 24- or 48-hour alert, missile crew members could not be expected to stay awake the entire time. To allow for sleep and rest, four-man crews were initially mandated. This meant that two members would be up and working while the other two could be in rest status.

Later, this practice was amended slightly, when the first solid-fueled ICBM, the Minuteman, was activated in the early 1960s. Tamper-indication seals were affixed to the control center's critical equipment drawers, allowing one crew member to sleep while the other stayed awake. Now, only two-person crews were required for each alert cycle.

Minuteman silos and launch control centers were constructed in Montana, Missouri, Wyoming and the Dakotas. Originally, Georgia and Texas had been considered for missile wings. However, when it was determined that the initial Minuteman range would be approximately 4,000 miles, the northern plains became the most suitable launching ground for the over-the-north-pole trajectories.

In 1963, the Air Force selected its sixth and final missile wing to be built in a 6,500-square mile area near Grand Forks Air Force Base, North Dakota. The new construction necessary for the missile wing was an economic boon for nearby Grand Forks. The city had first been established in 1874 as a trading post on the Red River. It had prospered and grown steadily over the years, servicing local farming communities and the air base.

Digging for missile silos and buried launch control centers began in spring, 1964 after the first thaw. About 5,500 construction workers made great progress over the warm weather months. Construction crews excavated sites for the buried control centers, then built an iron rebar frame that housed the capsule-like structure. After that, four-foot-thick concrete walls were poured, lined with a ¼-inch steel plate for the inner walls. Also, crews poured concrete for a 10-foot-square shaft that would house the elevator and access ladder, allowing crews to travel to and from the underground areas.

By 1966, all the facilities were completed, with 150 or so Minuteman missiles poised on strategic alert. This is the world that I was headed towards. Strange as it seemed, soon, I would know more about the inner workings of this system than the authors of the books I was studying.

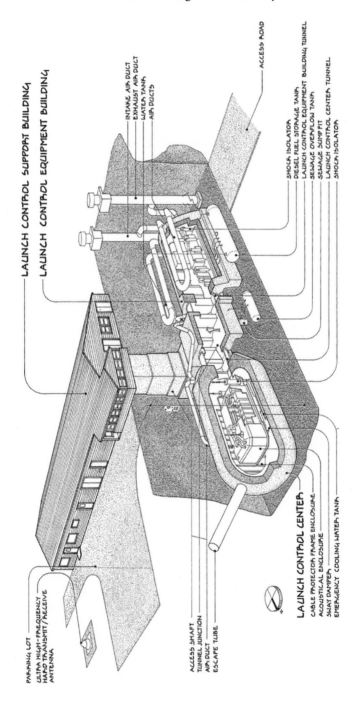

Diagram of a typical launch control facility (LCF). Although protected by security fence and armed personnel, the nondescript, above-ground buildings were easily viewed from public roads (Library of Congress, HAER, CO-84, sheet 4 of 4).

CHAPTER 7

The Pointy End Goes Up, Gentlemen

The central coast of California is an exciting place to spend three months. Unless those three months coincide with an intense 16-week course called Undergraduate Missile Training (UMT). It's hard to work on that tan while spending most of your daylight hours in a darkened simulator or windowless classroom. Even on weekends when Los Angeles beckons, so does your stack of Strategic Air Command technical orders, with countless checklists to be mastered by the following Monday.

A few weeks after OTS graduation I had successfully moved my wife and child out of our Oak Hill duplex and situated them at Beth's folks' home in the mountains north of Sacramento. Our reunion was much too brief, but like OTS, the first weeks of missile training would leave little time for family activities. I said my reluctant good-byes and drove four hours south to Vandenberg Air Force Base. Despite another family separation, I was excited to finally be starting my career as an officer. I wanted to make a good initial impression, get ICBM-smart, and then hit the ground running at my first missile base assignment.

Upon reporting in, I was once again assigned to temporary quarters on base, a single hotel-like room that shared an adjoining bathroom with another UMT student. Unlike officer training, I was free to come and go as I pleased. Vandenberg is a beautiful base with majestic cypress and eucalyptus trees, as well as over 30 miles of undeveloped coastline backed by green rolling hills. It's situated about 65 miles north of Santa Barbara on a jutting spit of land, which makes the weather quite windy and often foggy. The isolated area (I sense a theme here) is ideal for the base's primary mission, which is launching rockets to place national defense satellites in space.

In addition to the missile training school, there were several operational underground missile silos at Vandenberg. Each year, on-alert missiles were pulled from northern-tier silos, fitted with dummy warheads and shipped to California to be test-launched towards an uninhabited Pacific

35

island. This demonstration of the missile's accuracy was not only for the Air Force's benefit, but also for the spying Soviets to see that our capability was more than theoretical.

Off base, just minutes from these silos and launch complexes, were rustic Spanish missions, miles of farmland growing everything from garlic to oranges, and quaint little towns like Solvang and Los Olivos. Also nearby, tucked inconspicuously among the grassy hills was Neverland Ranch, the home of Michael Jackson. Of course, if you had a free weekend, Los Angeles was only a four-hour drive south along the spectacular coastline of Highway 1.

Unfortunately, most of my free time was spent digesting multiple binders crammed full with checklists and missile system component summaries. This was a brand-new world with its own terminology, equipment, processes and mindset. Therefore, no prior experience prepares you to launch ICBMs from an underground capsule. The Air Force accepted trainees from every civilian career field and academic discipline. I think their unofficial recruiting slogan was, "If we can teach a P.E. teacher to do this job, we can teach you!" Personally, I never noted any correlation between a specific undergraduate degree and success as a missileer.

Not that there weren't personal characteristics which made some trainees more suited for missiles than others. The ability to absorb a large amount of new information and arrange it logically in your mind for quick retrieval was a crucial skill. We were allowed to look up anything in our technical orders binders. However, there was rarely enough time, so a sharp memory was essential. I knew one lieutenant who supposedly had a near-photographic memory. Not surprisingly, he did very well in missiles. He went on to become a two-star general.

Another key trait was the ability to calmly focus in a loud, distracting and stressful environment. A launch capsule during war or any internal crisis is a cacophony of multiple alarms ringing, printers "ka-chunking" out messages, loudspeakers blaring codes and crew partners yelling directions at each other from ten feet away. You better have the ability to filter out what can wait and focus on what can't.

On my first day of Vandenberg training though, I didn't know what I was facing. My class consisted of twelve freshly commissioned lieutenants, most of whom had just graduated from college ROTC programs. Looking around the room, these young faces did not resemble the warriors you'd picture on the front lines of a nuclear war.

Like me, my classmates were motivated, energetic and anxious to make their mark. We developed almost immediate camaraderie, but also an underlying sense of competition. At 27 years old, I was the senior citizen in the class and the only student with a wife and child. My classmates immediately nicknamed me "Pappy."

We were to be trained in the more complicated of the two Minuteman III weapon systems. Nicknamed "Deuce," ours was the only system with both buried cable and medium frequency radio communications between control centers and their missiles. Other classes were taught either the older Minuteman II system or the one operating the Nation's newest missile, the Peacekeeper (MX). Each Peacekeeper was capable of carrying up to ten nuclear warheads.

Everyone in our class was eventually headed to Grand Forks Air Force Base, North Dakota, or to the single "Deuce" squadron at Malmstrom Air Force Base, Montana. Thankfully, no one in our class was sentenced to the most dreaded of all missile assignments—Minot Air Force Base. "Why not Minot? Freezin's the reason!" was a popular phrase. Minot was also in North Dakota, but Grand Forks was near a much larger town with a major university and nice shopping mall. It was also only 90 minutes from Fargo, the Big Apple of the plains. Minot was a much smaller town and a four-hour's drive from Fargo. If Grand Forks was purgatory, Minot was Hell.

At officer's training, I was permitted to submit for consideration my top three picks of desired missile base assignments. There were six bases to choose from. My top three were:

1. Whiteman Air Force Base in Missouri
2. F.E. Warren Air Force Base near Cheyenne, Wyoming
3. Ellsworth Air Force Base, near Rapids City, South Dakota

Grand Forks was fifth on my list and Minot was sixth. I might as well have told the Air Force I wanted a pony for Christmas. They assigned me to Grand Forks.

Wherever they were headed, all future missile launch officers, or "missileers" as we called ourselves, had their initial certification training at Vandenberg. Our four-month course consisted of three areas. First, there was weapon system classroom training which taught us about the Minuteman III missile, the launch control center (also referred to as the "LCC" or the "capsule"), our technical orders (checklists and guidance) and everything else we had to know in order to maintain our missiles in a day-to-day warfighting posture.

The second area was Emergency War Order (EWO) classroom training. This section gave us classified information about the procedures and checklists we would employ if ever called upon to launch our missiles. The thought of what we were being trained to do was sobering. However, at the time, my primary concern was doing well in the course.

The third training area was the most challenging: Missile Procedures Trainer (MPT) sessions. The trainer was a simulated launch control center where you and your assigned crew partner were thrown multiple real-life scenarios to put classroom training into practice. There were ten sessions or "rides" as we called them. Unlike amusement parks, these rides were rarely amusing and seemed to go on forever.

A typical session lasted over six hours including the in-brief and out-brief, where we were told in excruciating detail what we'd screwed up. It helped immensely to have a crew partner share the decision-making chores and to commiserate with when the session didn't go well. Which it often didn't. But before we were thrown in the simulator, or "box," we needed to first learn the basics.

The Minuteman III missile is not an especially intimidating rocket compared to its above ground counterparts. At a shade under 60 feet tall, it is less than a third the size of the Atlas V, Delta IV and Falcon 9 rockets which currently launch our nation's satellites into space. The Saturn V launch vehicle which carried the first men to the moon in 1969 was 363 feet tall—six times the size of a Minuteman.

Yet, big things come in small packages and the Minuteman III packs a huge wallop. The version I worked with could carry three independently targeted nuclear warheads. Each warhead was capable of yielding over 20 times the destructive power of the bomb dropped on Hiroshima in 1945. And it didn't take long to deliver that power.

Once launched from its underground silo, the missile quickly reached its maximum speed of over 15,000 miles per hour and could hit its overseas target in approximately 30 minutes. Since the Minuteman was a ballistic missile, it was similar to a fired bullet. Once aimed and released, its basic path could not be altered. In fact, after three minutes of flight, the boost engines shut down and it basically coasted the rest of the way.

Day to day, the Minuteman III sat in an underground silo at a fenced launch facility (LF), several miles from other silos. This dispersion made it harder for an enemy to take out several of our missiles with one of their own. Per its name, the missile was always ready to launch within minutes of being commanded. Ensuring this perpetual state of readiness was more of a safety issue with previous intercontinental ballistic missile versions.

For instance, the older Titan II model mated one control center with one missile, separating operator and rocket by only a short tunnel. Minuteman III launch control centers were several miles away from their missile sites. The Titan II was even more dangerous because, unlike the solid-fueled Minuteman, it was liquid-fueled. This made it more unstable, volatile and susceptible to accidents.

One 1980 Titan accident in Arkansas resulted in an explosion which killed an Air Force sergeant and wounded 21 other personnel. Fifteen years earlier, another Titan II fire killed 53 people on site. Neither accident involved the release of nuclear material, but solid-fueled or liquid-fueled, these missiles were dangerous entities, even sitting unarmed in their silos.

There was no room for inattention to detail or improvising when dealing with nuclear weapons. Our instructors let us know right away that that our every action would be meticulously directed, scrutinized and evaluated. As part of a two-person crew, we would control our assigned missiles from a submarine-shaped launch control center, buried about 60 feet underground. Each capsule controlled ten missiles in its active flight and monitored ten others controlled by another capsule. Five launch control centers controlled 50 missiles and made up the operations portion of one squadron. A single base's missile wing had three operational squadrons totaling 15 launch control centers and 150 missiles.

Supporting those missiles and operators in the field were missile maintenance personnel, security teams, cooks and facility managers. Almost all of them were enlisted personnel. Back at base there were code controllers, evaluators, instructors, commanders, etc., performing more administrative roles.

The missile sites were spread out over a large area encompassing a significant chunk of the state. Most were surrounded by security fences in small areas carved out of a farmer's field. Their locations weren't advertised, but they weren't hidden either, plainly visible from public roads.

What *was a secret* was what went on behind those chain link fences as the crews prepared for the President's launch orders. Our EWO training explained all that at the classified level. This meant that none of our lecture notes or training documents could leave the secure room after class. The upside was no homework, the downside was that any questions asked or studying had to be done in the secure, windowless facility. If you wanted to ask your classmate anything, it was NOT okay to whisper in his ear back at your base living quarters. Classified information was only allowed to be discussed in specific cleared areas. You could think about classified, though, anywhere you liked. As far as we knew, the Soviets did not have any mind reading machines.

In order to begin the EWO portion of our training, which started about three weeks in, we first had to get our Top Secret security clearances. For me, the clearance process had started back at officer training with an extensive questionnaire I was required to fill out. It asked for names, addresses and contact information of immediate family members, neighbors and close friends going back ten years. That information was then handed over to investigators who proceeded to check the veracity of the information by interviewing these same people, reviewing police records and searching for any incriminating information which might show me to be either untrustworthy or a possible target for Soviet blackmail.

The background investigation process can take some time, even for an Eagle Scout. For those students who had lived overseas, or had family or friends who were foreign nationals, it took even longer. If your background investigation had not been completed by the start of EWO training, you were essentially held back until either it was adjudicated satisfactorily or they found some significant negative information. At best, you waited for the next class to jump into, or at worst, if your clearance was denied, you were processed out of the Air Force.

Our mentors throughout this stressful time were our Vandenberg instructors. Most of them weren't much older than us, typically junior captains who had just completed their first four years of service as crew members. They were now assigned to Vandenberg attempting to cram their experience and time-tested techniques into our mushy skulls.

Some instructors were very easy-going and helpful. Others more tightly embraced the Strategic Air Command (SAC) reputation for "eating its young." To them, I'm sure we looked like cooked piglets lying on platters with apples stuck in our mouths. SAC was historically tough in its training requirements and strict adherence to step by step instructions. That makes sense when dealing with the unforgiving power of nuclear weapons. Those high standards began in the Command's early days, the tone set by the gruff and uncompromising SAC Commander, General Curtis LeMay.

There was so little room for improvisation that many disgruntled missileers referred to themselves as trained monkeys. "Read a step. Do a step. Get a Banana" was a sarcastic saying. Of course, the corollary to that was "Read a step. Mess up a step. Get whacked."

CHAPTER 8

The Box

There's a reason the Missile Procedures Trainer (MPT) is nicknamed "the box" and why a session inside is referred to as a "ride." Like the dreaded sweat box in prisoner of war camps, the trainer can be a place of unnerving isolation (there's that word again) and punishment. And, also like a theme park ride, there are ups, downs and surprises around every corner. When the seat harness is thankfully unbuckled, you stumble into the light, dizzy, disheveled and thankful the unpleasantness is finally over. Unlike a theme park ride, there is no waiting in line and the experience lasts for several hours. Neither of those attributes are a plus.

Our trainer was housed in a drab World War II–era wooden building that belied the high-tech simulator humming inside. Of course, "high-tech" for the 1989 Air Force meant 1960s cutting-edge technology.

Our class was told that, with a few exceptions, the trainer was a replica of a typical underground launch control center in North Dakota. As the day approached for our first session, we all felt a growing nervous anticipation. We would finally get to test our knowledge in what would essentially be our office for the next four years.

The twelve of us were paired off into two-person launch crews. For better or worse, we would be stuck with our crew partner for the duration of training. Speaking of better or worse, a crew partner assignment is essentially an arranged marriage. And like a marriage, there are couples who complete each other and couples who compete and fight with each other.

Head knowledge aside, the most important trait in a crew partner is a personality that meshes well with yours. Two strong and impulsive personalities will invariably butt heads, gloss over important details and blunder into bad decisions. Two cautious and deferential personalities will get bogged down in the details, work too slowly and miss the big picture. The best match is a strong leader willing to make quick decisions paired with a more deferential partner who sees details and keeps the crew from making a rash move.

My assigned crew partner was Lyle Ellis, a great guy, but unfortunately having a more cautious and get along personality like my own. We were both risk adverse (not a bad trait when dealing with nuclear weapons), detail-oriented and compelled to look at every angle before making a decision. We worked deliberately which frustrated our MPT instructor to no end. Here's a tip: To do well, avoid frustrating your instructor to no end.

Lyle and I may have been slow but we knew our stuff. Both of us were near the top of the class academically, seldom clashed and shared a wry, sarcastic sense of humor. The latter pulled us through some rough sessions. I'm a natural introvert but compared to Lyle, I was Robin Williams on speed. A taciturn single guy from Iowa, his idea of a temper tantrum was frowning.

Almost as important as the crew pairing is the MPT instructor assigned to each crew. Most crews respond better to a certain type of instructive approach than to others. Crews that are over-confident or too nonchalant, need an instructor to light a fire beneath them. Others, like the Ellis/Cook team, are naturally tough on themselves and respond better to an instructor who builds up the students' confidence.

As you might guess, the military in general, and Strategic Air Command specifically, do not produce instructors who excel in the art of verbal affirmation. Such as our MPT instructor, Captain Bland. The glass wasn't half-empty to him, it had a hole in the bottom.

Captain Bland wasn't a bad guy. He was smart and I'm sure an excellent missileer back in his crew assignment days. But he wasn't the best type of instructor for Lyle and me. He may have had an engaging personality in the office or at home, but he didn't bring it with him to the trainer. With a blank face and robotic voice, he would relentlessly recite our errors and warn us of impending doom in our final trainer evaluation.

My most vivid memory of Captain Bland is him staring at me with dead, unbelieving eyes while I stumbled through some procedure. His look said, "Your incompetence is beyond even my intellectual powers to correct."

Yet, Lyle and I knew none of this as we prepared for our first of ten trainer sessions. That initial morning, we excitedly dressed in our missile crew uniform of dark blue cotton pants and shirt with black boots. Around our necks we snapped a gold ascot, which for me was a never-ending irritant. Since it sat right below my chin, the ascot constantly chafed against my neck. Who can launch missiles with an itchy, sweaty neck? The darn thing also wouldn't stay in place. Halfway through a trainer session I would discover it had slid around to the back of my neck. My ascot had become a miniature cape. Not a professional look but frequently a sign of how the ride was going.

Besides ourselves, the most important thing we each brought into the trainer was our heavy brown technical orders case. More like a small suitcase than a briefcase. Inside, we kept a trio of three-ring binders with our unclassified checklists, diagrams, tables and equipment summaries. These were crucial to guiding us through the simulated scenarios thrown our way.

In the trainer, there was frequently a variety of events going on at once. That meant you might be simultaneously processing four or five checklists. It was easy to get confused about what step you were on for each. So, developing techniques to keep all your status straight was crucial. The best of these were passed down from missileer to missileer over the years.

An Army soldier's most crucial items might be a M16 and night vision goggles. Back then, a missileer's essentials were the grease pencil and a dozen clothes pins. Grease pencils were useful for checking off completed steps in your sheet protector–encased checklists or to mark clock times and write erasable reminders on your console's plexi-glass. Clothes pins were used to mark checklist pages that weren't complete so if you left to perform another action, you'd be reminded to come back to them. Without these items, the three technical orders binders and their hundreds of pages soon became a paper forest where a crew could quickly lose its way.

Each trainer session began with an introductory briefing from our instructor in a nearby classroom. Captain Bland would preview the general areas we would work on that day along with some advice on techniques to use. As industrious missileers, we were always looking for a newer, better technique. The best ideas hadn't changed for decades and almost everyone used them. Captain Bland was generally calm and positive while he imparted this wisdom. Lyle and I soon spoiled that attitude by about ten minutes into the ride.

After the in-brief, the three of us walked to the trainer entrance. Captain Bland punched in a key code to open the door. Security was tight because of the classified regulations kept inside for the Emergency War Order portion of the ride—the preparation and launching of missiles.

Once inside the door, we found ourselves in a small vestibule with radio music cranked up high. This was not for our entertainment but an anti-eavesdropping device to mask conversation inside the trainer. That first morning, we followed the captain forward through a second door into the actual simulated capsule.

At first glance, it was an overwhelming sight. In front of us was a rectangular room about 60 feet long and 30 feet wide. It hummed like a subway train preparing to leave the station. Stacks of electronics drawers formed facing rows of gray and green "high rises" with a narrow rubber matted walkway between them. The walkway formed a kind of circular track with electronics equipment on the inside and outside of the track.

Captain Bland led us forward towards the back of the trainer where on the far wall and back right wall two large consoles were arrayed in front of matching red cushioned chairs. These were the crew commander and status consoles. Both Lyle and I were training to begin our careers as deputies so we would take turns sitting in each position. I would be the deputy first and moved to the status console. We placed our various checklist binders, pencils and clothespins out on the small console tables and sat down in our chairs.

My keen powers of observation immediately noted that this was not your typical family room high-backed chair. Captain Bland verified this. "Gentlemen, these are the same chairs that bomber pilots have in their aircraft." *That explains the over the shoulder harness and seat belt*, I thought to myself.

"Wow, we get to sit in the cool guys' chairs," Lyle said with feigned awe. I laughed. Captain Bland stared at Lyle with a blank face.

Unlike the aircraft version, our chairs were attached to twin rails which, when a small release lever was pulled, allowed us to slide several feet down a row of equipment to check in-coming messages at a communications panel. Captain Bland encouraged us to practice this a few times. Sliding down the rail was kind of fun unless you failed to pull your knees in far enough and slammed them into the side of a sharp metal drawer at high speed.

Why were these chairs on rails? Because, as Captain Bland explained matter-of-factly, "During a war environment you need to be physically secured in case of a nearby nuclear detonation. Such a NUDET might topple over a free-standing chair, knocking you unconscious or otherwise causing severe injury. Then, you would be unable to complete the mission." Or, I thought, such a NUDET might more likely blow us to bits and not allow us to complete our life.

Looking up from my chair, I surveyed the status console. It was a confusing array of buttons, switches and flashing lights straight out of a 1962 science fiction film. Sensory overload. The experience was similar to looking at an airplane cockpit for the first time. Everything seemed an incomprehensible jumble of items vying for my attention. The only familiar sights were the telephone handset and the rotary dial. *Yes—rotary*. I wondered if I could call my old Air Force recruiter and ask him if it was too late to resign.

About twenty feet to my left and over my shoulder, Lyle was having a similar experience at the command console. Captain Bland was not fazed by our confused stares and methodically began to walk us through the equipment.

The deputy is the junior member of the two-person crew, and like the junior person at any job, is stuck with the grunt work. The deputy has phone buttons and a handset like the command console. However, the deputy also has additional equipment that the commander does not. For one, there are ten rows of lights behind plexi-glass. Each row corresponds to one of ten missiles controlled by the capsule. These missiles are in underground silos, five to ten miles away from the launch control center. Each missile's computer sends the control center its status via buried cables and, for redundancy, radio signal.

The color and blinking/not blinking status of illuminated light bulbs are all indicators of a missile's condition. In case the deputy doesn't have enough to look at, to the right of this array is another ten rows of missile lights. These represent the launch control center's passive flight, the ten missiles belonging to another control center. Our job is to also keep an eye on these missiles in case their primary crew does something wrong, or we need to take control of them in an emergency. So, a typical deputy must track 20 missiles at all times and actually has the capability to watch 50.

Since lights do not convey much detailed information, the Air Force has helpfully added another key piece of equipment at the status console—a paper printer. That sounds helpful until you learn that this printer does not print pictures or words, just three-digit numbers. These numbers, like a series of "300, 313, 319, 323, 341," tell a story about a problem the missile is having, a test it is processing, where it is in the launch commanded mode or possibly a security situation at the launch facility that needs to be reported.

The printer spits these numbers out constantly. They are essentially a foreign language the crew must memorize. Each one of these hundreds of three-digit numbers could be looked up in the technical orders binder. Yet, doing so would be like a tourist from Alabama trying to understand a fast-talking Paris street vendor by looking up each French word. You simply can't keep up that way.

You may wonder if it wouldn't be easier if there were cameras at the missile silos which could send real-time video to the capsules? Or, why not install printers which produce missile status in clear diagrams or plain English? Sure, but what would be the fun in that? Like everything else, those upgrades cost money. Also, my guess is that employing these obscure printer numbers was just another security precaution.

While the deputy is inundated with blinking lights, status change alarms and a printer that continuously vomits rolls of number-filled paper, the command console is a place of relative tranquility. Most of its controls deal with big war-making stuff: syncing computer countdown clocks, typing in missile target coordinates or inputting codes to enable the missile to accept a launch command. Since thankfully, most of those actions do not need to be accomplished most days, the crew commander has more time to digest the information the deputy is passing on, direct crew actions and see the big picture. The downside of not having a printer or missile lights is that

The status console at Oscar-Zero, where the deputy crew commander sat. At upper left is the red iron box where launch keys were kept (courtesy Peggy Weil and Fifer Garbesi–Emblematic Group).

commanders are almost totally dependent on what the deputy tells them. Bad information from the deputy means a bad decision by the commander which means a bad day for the crew.

Both commander and deputy have access to separate communications equipment from different sources. That way, if one source goes down, there are other means for military and national leaders to direct the launch crews. Both crew members have a switch that with their respective keys inserted and the missile in the proper configuration, will launch one or more missiles. That is, if they both turn keys almost simultaneously. Why those actions must be synched will be explained later.

After a couple hours of Captain Bland's show and tell, Lyle and I had enough situational awareness to be dangerous. It was time for our instructor to throw some scenarios at us. This initial portion of the trainer ride was dubbed "weapon system" and focused on our day-to-day job while on alert: ensuring that our launch control center and missiles were kept functional and ready for war. Captain Bland kicked the party off by walking to the back of the trainer and entering an elevated cab with smoked glass on three sides. Once seated inside, he could see everything we were doing below. At his disposal were computer tapes which triggered alarms, illuminated warning lights and commanded equipment racks to spew out data simulating actual situations a missile crew could encounter.

Lyle and I looked at each other with a nervous smile. Let the games begin.

CHAPTER 9

Riders May Experience
Slight Turbulence

A typical trainer session starts slowly. For instance, the topside flight security controller (FSC) calls down on the phone. He sounds suspiciously like Captain Bland. The FSC says the site cook is ready to enter the elevator shaft to deliver our dinner. Sadly, dinner is always simulated in the trainer. Before opening the topside security door, controlled from the capsule, we need to get a good authentication code from the FSC. The code lets us know he is not being coerced by a bad guy, or is not a bad guy himself, pretending to be the FSC. The FSC gets two shots at passing the correct code. He can only screw up once.

Uh oh. The FSC passes two bad codes in a row. No big deal. Something is wrong so we don't open the door. Now, however, we have a security situation which must be reported and investigated by an outside team. Lyle and I turn to that checklist and start working down the steps. We don't get very far before there's a jarring *Boom!* and the main capsule lights go out. We've lost primary power and the launch control center is switching over to battery power. Is this related to the security situation upstairs? We don't know yet.

There is a checklist for power changeovers. It will direct us to check circuit breakers and other equipment to see if there is an electrical issue. Do we work this electrical problem now or keep processing the security situation checklist? We've been taught to prioritize actions based on the "LESFO" principle. *Life* threatening issues first, then *Emergency War Order* (EWO) tasks, *security*, equipment *faults* (problems with equipment) and any *other* actions.

We decide to keep working the security situation. Once we've reported the security situation to base and are awaiting the response, Lyle and I clothespin the security checklist page as a reminder, then turn to our power changeover checklist.

We grab our flashlights so we can read in the dark and hurry to the other side of the capsule to check for tripped circuit breakers. We've barely begun when I realize I need a grease pencil to mark off steps. I run back to my console to get one. Apparently, while Lyle and I were huddled around the circuit breaker box, Captain Bland snuck in a problem with one of our missiles. Now on the status console, under the F-03 label, there are flashing lights. Also, the printer is spitting out row after row of three-digit numbers. Great, how long has that been going on? And, by the way, what is *that*??

OK, now we have three events going. Are they related? Which is more important to work first? Should we split up and work separate tasks or stay together? Is it too late to go back to teaching at Oak Hill?

As the events pile up, we know that through the smoky glass, right above our heads, Big Brother is watching. How bad are we screwing up? We will learn shortly because whenever we really fail, that cab door flies open and Captain Bland makes an appearance. This is the equivalent of a coach calling a time out in a basketball game. And like that brief interlude, Captain Bland uses his time to both berate us for whatever ever obvious mistakes we are making and to give us crucial guidance on how we untwist the pretzel of a situation we've gotten ourselves into. Regretfully for him, there are no substitutes to put in. Scott and Lyle are the only two players available.

There was little affirmation. To be fair, we gave him little to affirm. "Lieutenant Cook, I really liked how you answered the phone in a courteous manner. Lieutenant Ellis, good job walking to the back of the capsule without tripping over the chair rail."

And so it went for three and a half hours in a typical weapon system portion of a trainer session. There were cable breaks, equipment fires, security situations at various missile silos, equipment tests to run, communication messages to read, facility manager heart attacks to report, missile computers failing, maintenance teams which need to be processed on and off a missile site, and the never-ending alarms and flowing printer paper signifying every change of status. Another mundane day at the office.

Eventually, the sensory overload was ratcheted up several notches when we were trained in the classified procedures of actually launching the missiles. That was another one and a half hours added on to the end of a trainer session. Ninety minutes which were even more frenzied and stressful than the weapon system portion.

By the time Lyle and I trudged out of the trainer, we typically had been at it all morning with only one 15-minute rest room break. But we weren't done yet. Now we waited in an adjacent classroom for Captain Bland to write up his report. We used that time to speculate on our performance. Every conversation went something like this:

"I don't think that was too bad. Better than last time, right?"

"Sure. Maybe. I don't know.... What about that weird thing with the missile? You think that was related to the targeting thing?"

"No. I'm sure those were two totally different things."

"Well, we reported both things so I think we're covered."

"You know, I don't remember reporting the first thing. I know we talked about it, but..."

"No, we reported it. Right after that third thing. Or did, we...? Oh man, we're hosed."

"Maybe Captain Bland didn't notice that thing?" Lyle looks at me and arches his eyebrow.

One thing we both knew was that whatever the "thing" was, Captain Bland never missed anything.

About that time, Captain Bland would stride in the room, ready to walk us down memory lane. Event by excruciating event. He would point out in vivid detail what we did wrong and then balance his feedback by telling us what we did worse. By this time, I remember frequently feeling a mixture of depression, exhaustion and fogginess. It was difficult to focus on our critique.

It quickly became clear that even if the prospect of launching missiles was remote, pulling our monthly alerts would always be stressful. Just the daily responsibility of keep all ten of your missiles safeguarded, properly targeted and *ready* to launch at a moment's notice was a constant concern. Strategic Air Command boasted a missile alert rate of over 95 percent and accepted no less. That job expectation never eased up. We would have to adjust. It was part of the laborious process of becoming, what was affectionately called by our instructors, "SACumcized."

There were three daily trainer sessions available. The morning slot began at 6:00 a.m., which meant you had to be up by 4:30 a.m. That was rough, but by 12:30 you were free for the day. Technically. You were free to study even more hours with your crew partner, working on knowledge deficiencies or crew coordination issues. However, before doing that, I would often take a slow jog on Vandenberg's desolate beaches to clear my head. If you pulled the night shift, which started at 6:00 p.m., you were happy just to stumble back to your living quarters by 1:00 a.m. and fall into a deep sleep.

Those first few trainer sessions left Lyle and me feeling like we were the Tweedledee and Tweedledum of missile operations. As soon as we conquered one kind of problem, Captain Bland would throw in a new twist or move on to an issue we hadn't seen before. We wondered how our classmates were doing in comparison. No one wanted to be the crew bringing up the rear. We tried to subtly feel each other out, but that was difficult because other instructors had different standards and you never knew if your classmates were being honest about their trainer performance.

I might casually mention to Danny, a dry-witted Oklahoman who eventually would leave the Air Force to become an attorney, "Hey, that missile computer failure scenario in the trainer was pretty tough, huh?" If he said, "Yeah, we really botched that!" I'd feel a surge of satisfaction. *See, everybody's having problems.* If Danny said, "I don't know. We handled that one pretty smoothly," my heart would sink. *Lyle and I are the worst crew in the history of missile training.* Looking back, I'm sure that we were not nearly as hapless as we thought. And of course, Captain Bland was raised in a command culture where you break them down to … break them down some more.

There was one crew that I knew was having few problems in the trainer. Tony and Brent. They were the two sharpest students in our class. Both were extremely smart, seemed to ace all the tests and were invariably the first ones to pick up on new concepts.

Brent was one of those guys who knew he was smarter than you and didn't see any reason to pretend otherwise. Brent was a good guy though, very opinionated, but also willing to help anyone else who was struggling. Tony was a more self-deprecating and gregarious version of Brent. He was a chain-smoking, freckle-faced storyteller who would entertain you during study sessions with witty observations. It didn't seem fair that they were crewed together. It was like Babe Ruth and Barry Bonds put on the same team in a home run hitting contest. Yet, Brent and Tony were both so strong-willed that they frequently butted heads in the trainer.

While Brent and Tony argued over making a really good decision or a making a great decision, Lyle and I were frequently frozen in the land of indecision. The more Captain Bland harangued us, the more reluctant we were to make a move which might be wrong or bring another rant. So, we frequently discussed, and discussed, and discussed some more. Even if we were both convinced of the right move early on, we war-gamed what could go wrong and kept looking for ways we might possibly be tricked. Of course, this frustrated Captain Bland as our training sessions slowed down to a slog.

What we didn't realize until later, is that like a dance, a successful trainer session requires a certain flow and pace. Discussion is important, but it must be quick and keep up with surrounding events. Pace creates a back-and-forth rhythm between two people that actually cultivates clearer thinking, crisper actions and in the long run, better decisions. Invariably, initial thoughts are best and long "what if" sessions are more likely to talk you into an error, than out of one. Too much discussion also allows events to spiral so far ahead and outward that you lose control of them. We were taking a trainer ride like it was a written test instead of an evaluated action.

Halfway through our ten sessions Lyle and I had less confidence than when we began. Neither we nor Captain Bland were looking forward to our next ride. The three of us were trying to succeed in our own way, but were simply a bad match. Then, a miracle. In retrospect, it almost seemed like divine intervention.

Captain Bland was abruptly assigned to a supervisory job in the training squadron. It was a promotion for him and he appeared relieved to move on. Not as relieved as Lyle and I were. We were assigned a new instructor, Captain Javier Hernandez. A new start. But would the results be the same?

Captain Hernandez met with us the next week to introduce himself. He immediately presented a much more positive, friendly and laid-back personality than Captain Bland. He said that he had already reviewed our academic records and had actually watched our last trainer session from the cab. Lyle and I glanced at each other. Yikes. It had been an ugly one.

Captain Hernandez told us that he was excited to get a great crew. Lyle and I wondered which crew was that. Hernandez said we were both in the top five of the class academically which obviously meant we knew our stuff. He thought we were too risk-adverse in the trainer, though. Our reluctance to make a bad decision was holding us back.

He then made an astounding (to us) series of statements. "The trainer is just what the name says—training. You are supposed to make mistakes. I don't care as long as you are learning and trying not to make the same ones over and over again. If you make a mistake, no big deal. We'll discuss it and correct. I would rather you go faster and make more mistakes than get bogged down. If you go faster, you'll do better, I guarantee it. It's my job to help you succeed." That speech was like the sun emerging from behind a cloud.

Everything changed in the trainer after that. We still made mistakes but weren't afraid to anymore. Instead of our mutual anxiety feeding off each other, we fed off our instructor's positive attitude, regained our confidence and started moving forward like two in-sync pistons. We reacted faster and had more energy in the latter part of trainer rides.

Captain Hernandez knew how to break down concepts in ways we could understand them. He also gave us a guide full of techniques which he had accumulated over his four years on missile crew. They were good ones that I still used years later in Grand Forks. As a former educator myself, this new situation reinforced what I had always known—the right teacher can transform a student's trajectory. Wherever you are today, Captain Hernandez, thanks!

CHAPTER 10

Right Justified?

I didn't want to kill Russians. No missileer I knew of did either. The taking of another person's life is a sad and tragic thing, no matter the circumstance. Yet, I believed then, and still do, that there are circumstances where it may be necessary.

I wish that weren't true, that the world was different. I wish there were no such thing as nuclear weapons or wars. Yet, military members don't have the luxury of living in a theoretical, idealized or hoped-for world. We are forced to deal with the world as it is—flawed and filled with very real, dangerous, and aggressive evil. Someone has to raise his or her hand to do the dirty work of confronting that evil. It's not for everyone. But if we are to protect our loved ones and our freedom, it has to be for some.

A law enforcement officer might have to shoot a criminal who is in the act of attacking an innocent child. A fighter pilot may bomb a military target and, unintentionally, kill nearby civilians. Yet, for missile launch officers, there is a deeper and more disturbing reality.

No matter the military target, their missile will potentially kill untold numbers of innocent civilians.

Each missile launch officer has to search his or her own conscience about that fact. I can only speak from my own experience and reasoning. No doubt other officers have different perspectives. I also respect, yet disagree with, the many people who believe there is no rational or ethical justification to ever serve in this capacity. Many of my own relatives feel that way. They are good, smart people.

The Air Force recognized that this responsibility was one with which many missile students might struggle. To allow a frank exchange on ethics, our training schedule included a non-retributive discussion session facilitated by a chaplain. Without any instructors present, we were free to ask questions and air our concerns about the moral implications of launching nuclear weapons. This session took place soon after we began the classified Emergency War Order portion of our training. This benefited the Air Force by helping them identify conscientious objectors before more time and money was invested in their training. Likewise, this was our opportunity as trainees to make our reservations known so the Air Force could transfer us to another career field or, more likely, process us out of the service.

I don't remember anyone in our class raising deep concerns either in that discussion session or in private conversations. Did that mean there weren't any reservations? I don't know. However, by that point in training, we all had known for over a year that this was our career path. If any of us had second thoughts, we certainly had ample time to air them before missile training began.

The Air Force delayed this discussion session until after our initial classified briefings since this information might raise new concerns. It didn't for me. I never learned anything behind closed doors which gave me pause or made me lose faith in the ethics of my government. Which was a relief. We all want to trust the leaders giving us our orders, especially orders that direct such devastation.

The Air Force had other concerns. One was that, despite our pledging to turn keys, many of us might not do so when the actual order came down. I believe the Air Force assumed that a small percentage of missileers would refuse to launch in a real-world situation. Maybe some would believe that their own death was imminent and see little benefit in expanding the carnage. Other crew members might freeze when the horror of their task hit them for the first time. Even those without qualms could panic and slip up in their procedures. My guess was that the biggest percentage of those not turning keys would be officers who simply couldn't believe the order was authentic.

In reality, no one knows how they will react. I hoped that if the dreaded launch order came it would be preceded by days of heightened tensions. Then, I'd at least be mentally prepared. It would be hard not to hesitate if I received a launch message with no previous warning.

Of course, the greater day-to-day issue for the Air Force was whether or not a crew member was psychologically sound or a risk for blackmail or bribery. This determination was essential if these officers were to be entrusted with classified secrets.

Like everyone in a sensitive military position, missileers undergo extensive background checks before earning their Top Secret security clearance. Money troubles, mental health issues, crimes committed, illegal drug use, relationship problems, spousal abuse or sexual secrets were all blackmail vulnerabilities the government wanted to expose.

Because of the critical nature of the missile officer's task, it is paramount that the Air Force focus more stringently on their mental health. People who struggle with everyday life probably shouldn't be working in a buried capsule linked to nuclear-capable weapons. Also, crew members were issued firearms while on alert. Just another reason for increased scrutiny.

Part of this oversight was provided by the Personnel Reliability Program (PRP). Under this construct, there were strict rules about any medication that could be taken before or during alert duty. All missileers were directed to report any suspicious, depressive or erratic behavior observed in their coworkers or themselves. If there was any doubt about a missileer's state of mind, they were pulled from alert duty.

Before beginning their Vandenberg training, prospective missileers were required to pass an evaluation by an Air Force psychologist. For me, that appointment was scheduled while I was still teaching at Oak Hill. The nearest installation was Langley Air Force Base in Norfolk, clear on the other end of the state. That meant taking two days off from work.

As I drove across rural Virginia, I tried to anticipate what the psychologist might ask of me. Visions of ink blot interpretations, picture drawing and embarrassing sexual questions danced in my head. No matter what the doctor threw at me, I was determined to come across as *normal*, whatever that meant. I didn't trust psychologists and wasn't about to let this one scuttle my coveted officer training slot.

I needed to watch my non-verbals too. Excessive sweating or a high-pitched voice and he'd surely label me as weak or unreliable. Eye-twitching or reflexive giggling and I'd be written up as a prospective Unabomber. I could feel my anxiety rising.

By the time we began the interview, every nerve in my body was on heightened alert. After introducing himself, the psychologist asked how my trip down had gone. Alarms went off in my head. *Why'd he ask me that? What does he care about how my trip went? Maybe he's trying to get me to lower my guard. Or, maybe it's a test. Of what, though? What would be a "normal" response?*

I decided on, "It was fine. Thanks for asking."

He began writing on his notepad. *Oh no. I've blown it already. I should have expounded on "fine." Now he thinks I'm defensive or hiding details from him.* Before I could recover by offering additional trip details such as the McDonald's drive-through botching my lunch order, he threw out another question.

"So, I see you're going to be a missile guy. How do you feel about that?"

Uh oh. That nebulous "feel" word that psychologists love to use. How should a mentally stable person feel about being a missile guy? Proud? Excited? No, not excited! Ambivalent? Honored? My hands began to sweat so I stuck them in my lap.

I cleared my throat. "I'm, uh, glad to start my career. Missiles wasn't my first choice but I'm ready to do my best at whatever job the Air Force assigns me." *Good answer, Scott. A perfect balance between mission-oriented resolve and the reluctance of human compassion.*

The psychologist smiled and wrote more notes. *Hmmn. Was that an "I can't believe how normal and well balanced this guy is" smile, or a "I can't believe he tried to feed me that old patriotic line" smile?*

Before I could answer my own question—*Good grief, I was talking to myself! Quit that!*—he gave a follow-up. "Do you think you could turn keys and launch missiles if ordered to?" *There's only one answer to that question, right? It has to be "Yes." Unless it's a trick question....*

The psychologist raised an eyebrow as if to say, "*What's taking you so long? Are you conflicted?*" I blurted out, "Sure. I mean that's what I've signed up to do. Hope it never comes to that, but sure."

He nodded, expressing neither approval nor disappointment. More scribbling on the form. I tried unsuccessfully to read upside down. Finally, he stood up and extended his hand. "Well, I appreciate you making that long drive down. I'll finish this up later today and mail it out to your recruiter. He's in Bristol, right?"

Taken aback, I took his hand and sputtered an affirmation. It was over. I'd been in his office for no more than fifteen minutes. I quickly gathered my papers, stood and walked numbly out of the clinic. *I drove five hours and spent the night in a hotel—for that? How could he possibly know anything about me from two questions? Unless, maybe I was so normal that he realized there was no reason to probe farther. Yeah, that's it. Boy, I hope that's the reason.*

Apparently, I passed because I never heard about that meeting again. In the final analysis, the Air Force relied on me to do a job. I was on my own to determine just how I felt about that job. When I applied for Officer Training School, I didn't expect to be selected as a future missileer. But once I was selected, I began to wrestle with the moral questions it raised. I can't say I was ever totally comfortable with my conclusions. Yet, they were solid enough that I performed four years of missile duty with a clear conscience. My reasons may be simplistic or naïve to some, but they made sense to me. Like any good Air Force briefing, there are three main points:

1. By 1989, there were already thousands of operational nuclear weapons in the military arsenals of both the United States and the Soviet Union. Scott Cook wasn't going to change that. Both of our countries were working to reduce the number of missiles via the Strategic Arms Reduction Treaty (START) and other initiatives. That was going to be a long, slow process. In the meantime, my country needed competent officers to control their strategic weapons around the clock, ensuring there were no accidents or security breaches which might lead to

catastrophe. This daily safeguarding seemed like a noble vocation until that hoped-for day when all these missiles would be taken off alert.

2. Although theoretically possible, I never believed my country would launch these weapons unless we were already being attacked with similar fire power. I wasn't so sure about the Soviet Union. I didn't believe their leadership held the same respect for innocent life that ours did. So, in my mind, the best way to deter an attack was by our missile force being so skilled and resolute that our enemy would fear taking them on. An incompetent and reluctant United States missile force surely would not have the same effect. I know this idea is part of the "mutual assured destruction" concept for which many don't have much respect. Certainly, it's not ideal. Yet, until two countries no longer have missiles pointed at each other, I haven't heard a better plan articulated. I never thought unilateral disarmament was a safer way to go.

3. But what if deterrence doesn't work? What if the Soviet Union did attack us? Why launch then? Wouldn't this just kill more people needlessly? Without a doubt, more innocent people would die, although I trusted my government to target the aggressors—the Soviet military and their leadership. In those last moments I'm sure it would hit me that my family was probably already gone and I would be dead soon. The Soviets would target bases like Grand Forks and the surrounding missile fields. If the United States was being taken out as a world power, I would do everything I could to ensure the evil regime that had launched this unprovoked nuclear attack was not left to rule the world that remained.

Yet, in the end, I had an out. I never truly believed I would ever have to make these choices. The United States had only used nuclear weapons twice before, both attempting to force Japan's surrender in World War II. In the decades since, despite long, painful conflicts in Korea and Vietnam, through countless world crises and the Cold and Middle East Wars, we'd never used them again. I believed in my heart that the risk of being ordered to launch missiles was minimal.

CHAPTER 11

E(woe) Is Me

I imagine planning a nuclear war must be similar to directing a Broadway musical. You have multiple actors, singers and dancers, each with specific skills that need to be coordinated. One group has to make its entrance at just the precise moment so as not to step on the lines or actions of other performers already on stage. Once on stage, each cast member must efficiently move about a limited space, ensuring they do not bump into others or delay them from hitting their marks.

The United States' war planners have similar challenges on a much grander and more somber scale. Any release of nuclear weapons involves detailed coordination of forces from each military service. In ordering a nuclear missile strike, that means close coordination in targeting, platform position and weapon release times among the Air Force's bomber aircraft, the Air Force's land-based strategic missile sites and the Navy's fleet of nuclear weaponized submarines. For instance, you don't want bomber aircraft in the vicinity of a Minuteman III flying in towards its nearby target. Nor would you want two missiles impacting so close that their intended effects are significantly altered by the other.

Besides the initial planning, there has to be real-time follow-up to determine what targets were hit, which of our forces were taken out before they could perform their missions and what weapons are left in the arsenal to strike the targets that remain.

Theoretically, a launch order could come without warning. However, the more likely scenario was that such an order would follow a gradual build-up of tensions between the United States and an adversary. As war became more likely, Strategic Air Command forces would be placed in higher defense readiness conditions, or DEFCONS. These conditions, numbered from 5 (lowest) to 1 (highest), would give missile crews a sense for how close they might be to hostile action.

Yet, once the launch order came down, missile crews would be fairly oblivious to what the enemy or our own forces were doing. That's for the best. Their only concern is properly executing their piece to this puzzle. That means decoding messages, determining an authentic order and launching missiles in the correct number and timing specified. A Top Secret security clearance does not give the possessor the right to see the entire war plan. In general, classified information is meted out on a "need to know" basis. If you do not need certain facts to do your specific job, you probably won't be given them.

Conspiracy theorists are naturally cynical of this practice. Many would say this compartmentalization is an excuse to keep the junior troops in the dark so unethical leaders can manipulate them into performing actions they normally wouldn't do. I grant that is a risk. There is no doubt that such a system places great trust in the planners and leaders who determine what orders will flow downward.

Yet, from a security standpoint, it makes sense to limit military members' knowledge of classified information. Protecting classified information is hard enough with the thousands of military personnel who actually need it to perform their missions. Opening up these secrets to people who simply would *like to know* creates an unnecessary compromise risk. Each new person added to an access list presents one more vulnerability. One more point where sensitive information could be leaked either intentionally or through error.

I didn't understand the "need to know" concept at first. Thus, I had unrealistic expectations about what doors my security clearance would open for me. I had visions of learning where the Air Force was keeping the captured aliens or which members of Congress were suspected Russian spies. To launch my missiles I didn't need to know that the recovered alien corpses were kept in a bunker beneath an abandoned Denny's restaurant in Montgomery, Alabama (not true by the way). Our classified briefings in training were strictly missile operations stuff. While somewhat interesting, this information wouldn't necessarily send a thrill up the leg of a conspiracy theorist.

While on crew, occasionally we were given a fascinating glimpse at strategic planning several levels above us. However, those briefings were rare and more intended as a morale boost. I assumed they thought we would be more motivated to drive out to the launch control center eight times a month if we had more insight into our role in the bigger war plan.

Obviously, what we did learn, I can't talk about. We were incessantly warned about the consequences of either deliberately or accidently allowing these secrets to get into the hands of non-cleared individuals. The non-disclosure forms we signed were more unsettling than a gas station bathroom. It was all warnings about prosecution to the fullest extent of the law, fines in the thousands of dollars, loss of rank, humiliation and of course, long prison terms where we would be forced to dig and re-fill holes for the rest of our adult life. It was clear that little sympathy would be shown to anyone who messed up in this area.

It wasn't easy to keep all that sensitive information straight, though. Each day at missile training we were being taught both classified and unclassified content. As much as we tried to keep the two clearly separated in our minds, at times they tended to bleed over. When asked about our studies by families and friends we learned to think before speaking and when in doubt, not speak at all.

To tax our feeble brains even more, some facts were unclassified by themselves, but became classified if you affiliated them with another specific fact. So, you also had to know which combinations would get you in trouble.

We relied heavily on each other. Several times I remember being pulled aside at some social function by one of my classmates and having a conversation like this (whispering in my ear):

"You know those things we learned last week about that process?"

"Yeah."

"That's not classified, right, to say that one thing is part of the other thing?"

"Yeah, I think it is, actually."

(wincing) "Really? You sure?"

"Yes. I remember Captain Jones saying that specifically. Why? You didn't tell anybody about that, did you?"

"Oh no. Just asking. Just asking."

I imagine that lieutenant then hustling away to the potluck dessert table and cornering his girlfriend. "Hey babe, you know that thing I just told ya? Don't ever repeat that, okay? That might be a little, you know, sensitive. And especially don't ever tell anyone I told you that." But I'm sure that never happened.

Once all these sensitive plans and procedures were locked away in our brains, we were once again called upon to demonstrate our understanding in the trainer. The Emergency War Order (EWO), or missile-launching section, was always the last section of a ride. In this environment, procedures and decisions built on one another so an early mistake could begin a chain of unfortunate events. A fault light or print-out is missed so a missile problem doesn't get fixed. Since the missile doesn't get fixed, it never properly aligns for launch. Since it doesn't align for launch, it doesn't launch later when ordered to. The target it was responsible for doesn't get destroyed. That target was a Russian ICBM aimed at your flight of missiles. Oops. Here it comes. On the positive side, you don't have to worry about working that tricky escape tunnel hatch. It won't even be there in 20 minutes. And neither will you. Have a nice day.

Yet these real-life scenarios were not in the forefront of my mind or Lyle's. We just didn't want to botch the trainer ride. Captain Hernandez was a nice guy, but he was still a Strategic Air Command instructor. He wasn't going to let an incompetent crew slide.

If you have trouble focusing amid noise and chaos, an EWO training ride session will be a challenge. In fact, possibly the best missileers would be parents of small children whose daily lives are nothing but noise and chaos.

The distractions begin with the capsule's multiple communications equipment. Each has their unique annoying alarm that blares whenever a message is received. And in EWO, every printer seems to be spitting out redundant messages in machine gun fashion. Again, this is by design. If one communication link goes down, senior leaders can still get directives out to the crews through at least three other modes.

Because the communications equipment is located to the sides of the status and command consoles, crew members have to frequently pause their actions to slide down and check messages. More often than not, these messages are a redundant copy of one that arrived earlier.

I say "slide down" because in EWO, both crew members are strapped into their respective chairs. That means to talk, Lyle and I are forced to yell at each other over the din. As you can imagine, it's sometimes difficult to hear what a crew partner is saying. Adding to the headache is the loud system printer at the status console, phones ringing and launch facility status change alarms going off at both consoles.

The most stress-inducing messages are those received by voice piped into the capsule. Those announcers are usually reciting important alphanumeric letters which must be copied down exactly and decoded. "Alpha, Tango, Juliet, Bravo, Bravo, Sierra, Foxtrot…. I say again…. Lima, Alpha,…." When those messages begin, you better move fast. A message may only be repeated once. There is no copying someone else's work in the capsule. For decoding and other actions each crew partner must independently determine what is being directed.

Crews can't communicate with the "Voice." There is no "Wait, can you repeat that a third time?" or "Hold on, I just dropped my book on the floor and all the pages fell out of the binder." The Voice is somewhere in Strategic Air Command Heaven and is speaking to many capsules. He does not know and does not care what problems Lieutenant Ellis and Lieutenant Cook are having in their little world.

Jerry Seinfeld once said that there is no panic bigger than being in someone else's bathroom, flushing the toilet, then seeing the swirling water rise and rise and rise. A close second might be copying down a crucial 22 letter message to be decoded and realizing that you copied down 23 letters and have no idea where you got off track. And by the way, there are 32 seconds left to perform your actions before you and your crew partner decide to launch missiles—or not.

Many crew actions in the EWO portion of a ride are timed. That's why the clock over the command console is so important and must be daily calibrated with the Naval Observatory in Washington, D.C. A crew must not only launch within a certain time limit after receiving an order, but they must launch precisely at the time directed. Early is just as bad as late. Similar to your entrance in a play, to return to my earlier analogy.

If a crew busts a crucial time limit in EWO, even by a few seconds, it's considered a major error in a training ride. If they bust a crucial time in a formal evaluation, like the one to graduate from missile training at Vandenberg, they fail the entire evaluation. If they bust their time in a real war, thousands of innocent U.S. citizens may die.

To get to those crucial moments before launch, missiles need to be prepped. Day to day, a missile sits "locked" in its silo. It can't accept a launch command until its computer is "unlocked" with an enable code. Lieutenant Cook and Lieutenant Ellis do not have the enable code for obvious reasons. That code is only released by higher authorities. To create the complete enable code, the crew commander takes certain numbers and enters them into switches on his console. He or she then turns a lever which then either arms a specific missile or all ten of them in the flight.

Soon after that, the crew may be ordered to prepare for launching the missile by retrieving their launch keys out of a locked iron safe above the status console. The safe door is secured by two combination locks, each owned by one crew member. They do not know their crew partner's lock combination. Keys are retrieved and inserted into the launch panel at both consoles.

There is a lot going on, but a simplified version is this. When a legitimate launch order comes down from the President, both crew members simultaneously turn keys in a rehearsed script they could perform in their sleep. The two console key slots are located far enough apart so one person could not turn both keys at the same time.

COMMANDER: I have a legitimate launch order and a time of XXXX?
DEPUTY: I agree.
COMMANDER: (staring as the second hand sweeps around on clock) We are 35
     seconds away.
DEPUTY: Yes. I agree.
COMMANDER: 20 seconds. Hands on keys (they both reach out and grip their
     respective key, still staring at the clock).
COMMANDER: I'm in cable mode. On my mark. 3–2-1. Key turn! Release.
DEPUTY: Released.

COMMANDER: I'm in radio mode. On my mark. 3–2-1. Key turn! Release.
DEPUTY: Released.
COMMANDER: Deputy, read me your indications.

At that point the focus is back on the deputy, since the status console displays the individual missile lights. He or she begins reading off indications so the commander can determine if everything that was supposed to, accepted the launch order. "I have launch commanded for LFs F-01, 02, 04, 06, 08. I have Missile Away lights for…."

For any of that to happen, another crew must also have turned keys successfully. Remember, it takes four crew members turning keys to launch each missile. The time from a missile receiving a legitimate launch vote until it flies out of the silo can be less than 90 seconds.

Although multiple missiles can simultaneously receive a launch order, they don't necessarily launch at the same time. Some missile computers have a longer delay built in. This is partly a precaution to avoid placing too many weapons in the same air space and impacting each other's flight paths or detonations.

While all this was going on, you couldn't forget about monitoring your secondary flight of ten missiles, under the primary responsibility of another capsule crew. If that crew tried to enable or launch their missiles when not authorized, you were required to send out an Inhibit command which would temporarily cancel those illegal commands and prevent their missiles from launching.

These frequent dress rehearsals for Doomsday could be wearing. As missile students, we looked forward to our weekends. Those too few hours with family and loved ones offered much-needed relief from the pressure of studies. What better place to decompress than the central coast of California?

CHAPTER 12

California's Endless Fall

Halfway through my missile training, Beth's folks drove her and Brett down from Northern California. Beth's dad, a retired Air Force Chaplain, and his wife Doris lived in the mountains near Sacramento. Beth and Brett had been staying with them, allowing me to concentrate on my studies.

Now that I had settled into a routine, my in-laws pulled their trailer down so the four of them could stay at the on-base Family Campground. These areas are typically populated by silver-haired retirees living in battleship-sized recreational vehicles (RV). Some of these travelers spend much of their golden years driving from base to base, soaking in the nostalgia of their active-duty time.

At Vandenberg, spouses weren't allowed to live in the assigned on-base student quarters. I wanted to be with Beth, so I moved into her folks' trailer. Compared to the RV armada surrounding us, my in-laws' trailer was more of a patrol boat. Space was tight for five people, especially at 4 a.m. when I dressed for my early trainer session. On those mornings, I moved cautiously in the dark, trying not to stumble over the four other sleeping bodies.

On clear days, most campers fled their wheeled homes to enjoy leisure activities in the warm California sun. But more often than not, the sun was a no-show. Vandenberg Air Force Base sits out on a jagged coastline, four hours north of Los Angeles. This geographic location frequently brings weather that is more reminiscent of San Francisco than San Diego. It was frequently foggy in the morning and then grew windier as the day wore on. Temperatures typically hovered in the low to mid-sixties. When the sun went down, so did the temperature—dramatically.

At least our trailer had solid walls and heating. Not so for all our neighbors. One poor staff sergeant wrongly assumed that California was all summer, all the time. He brought his wife and three kids with him for a two-month training course. His plan was to save on hotel expenses by living at the Family Campground in a pop-up camper with mesh siding. And no heat. They froze the first few nights before some sympathetic RV neighbors brought them donated winter coats and an electric heater. The sergeant's wife, though pleased with the hospitality, was not happy with her husband's lack of weather research. However cold it was in their camper it was even frostier between the two of them.

Beth and I had experienced a few marital Cold Wars. Yet, during our early years of marriage, we had also bonded through a couple tough experiences. One of those was Brett's birth. At the time, we had been married for four years and were both working as teachers at Oak Hill Academy. The timing seemed right to expand our dynamic duo to a trio. Getting pregnant has never been a problem for us and Beth's first seven months of nesting went without a hitch.

One Saturday morning though, she discovered some unexpected leaking. Concerned, yet too naive to be alarmed, we quickly dressed and I drove her 30 miles to the doctor's office in Galax. Beth was taken back to see the doctor while I found a seat in the lobby.

After 15 minutes, I was called back and found Beth sitting in a chair crying. The doctor explained that her water had broken at home. She was probably going to have the baby. "You mean, like today?" I said in disbelief. Yes, like today.

They put her on a gurney and transported her to the adjacent county hospital. There, they attempted to stop her labor, but couldn't. The next piece of alarming news was that they now needed to transport her via ambulance to a larger hospital in Roanoke. "We don't have the facilities to care for pre-mature babies here," the doctor explained. I was stunned. Roanoke was a two-hour drive away. Was that safe? Was Beth going to be all right? What about the baby? We'd left the house with nothing but the clothes on our backs. I was told that I couldn't ride in the ambulance with her and besides, I would need my car in Roanoke.

As a group of nurses prepped Beth for transport, I sprinted to the car, flew down the road to a gas station and fueled up. I barely made it back before the ambulance took off for the interstate with Beth and a nurse inside. My mind was reeling. I was going to be a father—today! We were scheduled to begin Lamaze classes the following week. I wished I'd read that new baby book Beth had received in the shower the school ladies had thrown for her. I drove fast and prayed faster.

As we approached Roanoke, the ambulance sped up. I tried to keep pace and strained to see what was going on through the ambulance's small back window. Was my wife giving birth in there? I didn't want to have the first glimpse of my child while driving 90 mph on Interstate 81.

We arrived in Roanoke soon after. The ambulance whipped around the side of the hospital to the Emergency Room entrance. They hurriedly wheeled Beth inside as I skidded into a nearby parking space. I just made it to the elevator as a couple orderlies and a nurse pushed Beth's gurney inside. I held her hand and tried to look confident. Jammed in with us was were several peach-faced interns, looking like they were on a college field trip. They must have been summoned to watch as part of their medical training. I wasn't thrilled that our crisis was supplying the afternoon's entertainment. I squeezed Beth's hand and stroked her hair. She was calm, although obviously shaken and in real pain. I admired her grit but wished there was something more I could do to reassure her.

When we reached the maternity floor, they wheeled Beth into the delivery room. An orderly tossed me a pair of scrubs. "Hurry up, or you'll miss it," he said. I slung the blue pajamas on, fastened the medical mask over my face and hurried next door. They were already exhorting Beth to push. Within minutes, here came Brett, red, scrawny, but crying and very much full of life. I was joyful, relieved, but still concerned. They allowed Beth to hold Brett briefly then hustled him off to the preemie unit to be hooked up to an array of sensors and an oxygen mask. It was barely five hours from the moment when we had left our house 150 miles away for a doctor's visit.

The next few weeks were a whirlwind of activity and emotions. Brett was born almost six weeks early. His health issues kept him in the hospital's preemie unit for almost a month. When he was finally released, Beth and I were understandably nervous. One day our son has nurses hovering over him and machines monitoring his vitals around the clock. Then, the next day, they say "Here, you go!" and the care for this fragile life is now in our very inexperienced hands.

We were extremely cautious and handled Brett like a bomb about to go off. We must have taken 15 minutes just carefully securing him in his car seat. I think I drove about 20 mph all the way home, spending more time checking Brett in the rear-view mirror, than traffic out the front. That kind of experience bonds a couple. I sometimes wonder what the impact would have been on our marriage if Brett's birth had turned out differently.

Now at Vandenberg, a couple years later, Brett looked as big and healthy as any other two year old. Except of course, that he was clearly more handsome, brilliant, talented and athletic. Just stating the obvious.

It was wonderful to have my wife and son with me those final weeks of class. On weekends we took some family time to visit nearby sights like the La Purisima Mission and quaint little towns like Solvang and Buellton. On farther jaunts we toured Hearst Castle up north and the Santa Barbara Zoo and Universal Studios in Los Angeles down south. On our Universal Studios tram tour, we drove through a just-completed movie set, the town square for upcoming *Back to the Future II*.

Back on base, there were miles of almost deserted beach to explore. No swimming though. The water was freezing and dangerous currents could easily drag unsuspecting swimmers out to sea, never to be seen again. So, we settled for wading in the dozens of tide pools dotting the rocky coastline. The scenery was stunning. I wondered how many millions of dollars developers would pay for the opportunity to build expensive homes and luxury resorts on this pristine land. The current beach residents were a smattering of launch complexes, some wild birds and rare nesting turtles. Anyone caught disturbing the nest of one of the latter was liable for fines in the tens of thousands of dollars.

One of the more spectacular man-made sights on Vandenberg was Space Launch Complex 6. It sat at the edge of the base's coastline, built up against a high sloping hill. Just below its fence line, ocean waves crashed onto the jagged rocks. It was built to be the West Coast launch site for NASA's space shuttle. However, after the 1986 Challenger accident, the entire program was re-evaluated, and NASA decided to not expand shuttle launches to Vandenberg.

California is a beautiful state. I couldn't help but imagine though, what would be left the day after a nuclear war? Sometimes I was so caught up in my training that it was easy to forget the real-life impacts of the war I was training for. The thought was almost unimaginable. When out at a local restaurant, I wondered what the other diners would think of me, if they knew what I was training to do. Would they hate me? Did any of them give one moment's thought to the possibility of a nuclear war? I doubt many of them spent time worrying about it. That was probably for the best.

As our final days of training approached, I was ready to move on. I wasn't anxious to leave California for North Dakota. I was tired though of living in a small trailer with my wife, son and in-laws. I was ready to begin doing my job and settling into a house our little family could call home for the first time in a year.

Lyle and I finished training with academic averages near the top of our class. The one obstacle remaining was to pass an end of course trainer evaluation. If we failed it, we weren't going to North Dakota or anywhere else soon. That final evaluation would be administered, not by our instructors, but by officers from SMES—the 3901st Strategic Missile Evaluation Squadron. These were the black hat guys who didn't smile. Their judgment would be final.

Captain Hernandez did his best to get Lyle and me to relax. "You guys have nothing to worry about," he'd say. "Just stay together during the simulated events, work through your tech data and you'll be fine. They won't show you anything in the evaluation you haven't already seen and handled easily in training. I'm not worried at all."

Of course, he wasn't. We would be under the gun, not him. Our final trainer session was straightforward, no doubt intended to bolster an anxiety-filled crew's confidence going into the evaluation. Afterwards, Lyle and I met for a couple of marathon study sessions. Our goal was to anticipate every scenario the SMES evaluators could throw at us.

The night before the evaluation, I barely slept. Not a good way to prep for the four most critical hours of my fledging Air Force career.

Turns out we had nothing to worry about. The evaluation was not as difficult as I anticipated. We only made a couple of minor errors—none in EWO. When our final course scores were calculated, both Lyle and I earned Distinguished Graduate status. It was the highest honor awarded. That distinction would accompany us to our first duty assignments and be a highlight of our first annual officer performance reports. I was more relieved than ecstatic.

We were amazed at finishing so well considering how much we'd floundered at the outset. I thanked Lyle for sticking with me during those first weeks in the trainer. We never fought or undermined each other like some other crews had done. We stayed focused on improving as a team and it had paid off.

Lyle was one of three in our class headed for Malmstrom Air Force Base in Montana. The other nine of us would reunite in a couple weeks at Grand Forks Air Force Base in North Dakota. I only saw Lyle one time after that, years later when we were both majors. I've lost track of him since. He wasn't the kind of guy to cultivate social ties outside of work. No matter. Like my officer training classmates, he and I will always share a very significant emotional event in our lives.

I was proud to have successfully passed the twin gauntlets of officer training and missile training. Yet, it was becoming clear that earning respect within my new profession would be a never-ending process. Respect wasn't a medal pinned on me the first day I donned a uniform. It couldn't be boxed up and carried with me from assignment to assignment.

I was now moving to my third base in twelve months. My future career would be similar with new assignments every three to four years until retirement. At each new stop I'd learn that the accomplishments and status of my previous assignment meant little at the new one. My new peers and bosses only cared about the job I was doing for them. My new assignment in Grand Forks would be no different. To my new squadron, a Distinguished Graduate designation was just a line on a piece of paper. If I had any skill, I'd need to prove it to them in a real-life launch control center. Square one—again.

CHAPTER 13

Go North, Young Man

If you want to fight a Cold War, what better place than North Dakota? Nobody does cold like our 39th state. I read that the average January high in Grand Forks tops out at an invigorating 15 degrees Fahrenheit. The average low is -2 degrees. If you were lucky enough to be at Grand Forks Air Force Base on that record-setting day in January of 2004, you would have basked in an unbelievable -40 degrees, -60 degrees wind chill.

Be warned, the North Dakota Board of Tourism is quite sensitive to jokes about how cold it is in their beloved state. On their web site, they attack these misconceptions by pointing out that North Dakota's average winter temperatures are only six degrees colder than Chicago's and ten degrees colder than Boston's! And, once you've lost the ability to change facial expressions, what's a few degrees colder? Although an admirable effort, I'm not sure this type of marketing will send Mr. and Mrs. Joe Public scurrying to pack for a northern-tier vacation.

Military members don't have a choice. When we get orders, we pack. So, Beth and I loaded up the Ford Tempo, said our goodbyes to friends at Oak Hill Academy and set out for North Dakota. Somewhere in the back seat, squeezed between suitcases, food containers, shoes, toys, diapers, hanging uniforms and military training materials was a small car seat holding our son. We couldn't see Brett but knew he was there because of all the crying.

I pointed the car north and made a mental note to turn around if I approached a sign saying *Welcome to Canada*. Mountains turned into hills and by the third day, hills had given way to vast flat open spaces. There seemed to be nothing but farmland stretching to the horizon in all directions. I remarked to Beth that I couldn't remember the last curve in the highway. The weather turned bleak and each mile marker seemed to summon a deeper gray and more snow flurries. Beth reached over and squeezed my hand. Was that a gesture of affection, fear, or a subtle way of saying, "This might be a bigger mistake than you trading away my Fiat"?

There wasn't much to see outside the windshield, so Beth began reading me fun facts about our new home. North Dakota was the *least* visited state in the union. It has snowed there in every month except July and August. North Dakota produces enough soybeans to make over 4 billion crayons each year. *Take that, New York!* Nearly 90 percent of North Dakota land area is in farms and ranches. *Eat your heart out, Texas!* The geographical center of North America is Rugby, North Dakota. Curious, nothing about Rugby being the economic or cultural center of anything.

When Beth breathlessly revealed that North Dakota was home of the world's largest buffalo statue, I'd had enough. Maybe we could play the alphabet game instead? Two hours later with few passing license plates to observe and fewer billboards, we abandoned that competition, both stuck on "Q."

A little after 8:00 that night, we exited the highway into Grand Forks. This was a metropolis compared to the many rural towns we had passed since crossing the border. Those were typically small clusters of drab homes and a single church huddled around tall grain silos next to railroad tracks. Here there were multi-story buildings, fast food places, hotels, an indoor shopping mall and the University of North Dakota—home of the Fighting Sioux. The base lodging facilities were booked for the night so my plan was to grab a hotel room in town. It had been a long day on the road and Brett wasn't the only cranky Cook.

The first hotel we stopped at was full. I thought that was odd for a non-holiday weekend and little interstate traffic. The second hotel didn't have any rooms either. Neither did the third. *What was going on?*

"Is there a convention in town?" I finally asked one of the clerks.

"No," he sniffed, as if I was implying that an establishment like his couldn't be full. "This is pretty typical for us on a weekend."

I was incredulous. *Who were these people and what were they doing in Grand Forks taking my hotel room?*

After striking out at two more motor inns, I concluded that apart from the seedy rent-by-the-hour variety, there was not a hotel room to be had in all the city. It was now almost 10:00 p.m. with a temperature of a similar number. In desperation, I found a pay phone and called a married missileer friend who was already in base housing. Could we possibly crash on his floor for the night? He said sure and explained to me that the hotels were full of Canadians. The currency exchange rate was so good that they flocked down here on weekends, loading up on K-Mart and other retail store purchases by day, drinking beer by night, then heading home on Sunday.

Once again, I was stunned. How bad must life be in Winnipeg if your big getaway is a wild weekend in Grand Forks, North Dakota? An over two-hour drive from home, no less. North Dakota may have been the least-visited state in the union, but apparently Grand Forks was a shining exception. As I curled up on the musty sofa in my friend's basement, I sensed that the Cooks were about to embark on a strange new journey.

The next morning, we thanked our hosts then headed over to the base lodging office. There, we were handed the keys to one of their temporary lodging apartments. These were set aside for arriving military members and their families until they could find permanent housing. Our apartment was basically a trailer with an accordion partition separating the living room/kitchen area from the bedroom. Beth began setting up house while Brett excitedly raced around the small space, excited to be free of his car seat.

I hung up my service dress coat and carefully affixed my only two ribbons (training and expert marksman), name tag, and second lieutenant bars, all according to regulation. I then ironed my blue dress shirt, undershirt and pants, careful to get the creases just right. I was to report to my new commander the next morning and wanted to make a good first impression.

Once settled in, we decided to take a little windshield tour of our new surroundings. The base sat out on the prairie, 15 miles from town. As we had driven towards it the night before, its lights and perimeter security fence gave the illusion of a state penitentiary. San Diego Naval Station this was not. However, in the light of day, it revealed itself to be, although bereft of any physical beauty, a typical military base.

At the west end stretched a large runway and several huge hangers with sleek, black B-1 bombers either lined up out front or being worked on inside. I knew these aircraft were built to carry nuclear weapons. Their crews, similar to missileers, pulled alert duty. They were poised to take off within a moment's notice and fly across the ocean to hit targets in places like the Soviet Union.

Just east of the flight line was the usual mix of administrative and maintenance buildings. The rest of the base consisted of recreational and personnel support facilities. Military installations, like a small town, are almost entirely self-sufficient. A family could never set foot outside the gate and still live a comfortable life.

We drove by the small base hospital, complete with a maternity ward, pharmacy and 24-hour emergency room. Nestled among a large section of homes were not one, but two elementary schools, testifying to the many young families living on base. We noted a base chapel, gymnasium, commissary (grocery store), exchange (retail store), Burger King, Officer's Club, gas station, childcare center, movie theater and the two facilities no military base ever seems to be without—a golf course and bowling center. Not bad. Beth was anxious for us to get on the waiting list for a base house, though. I promised to do that after reporting to my squadron the following day.

At 7:00 a.m. the next morning, careful not to awaken Brett and Beth,

I quietly donned my service dress uniform, slipped on my dress shoes and grabbed my flight cap. I stepped out the front door and was greeted by twin surprises. First, a freezing wind that pierced me like a thousand blow darts from a tribe of pygmies. I felt like I'd been hit with a taser. It was so cold, I reflexively glanced down to ensure I was actually wearing clothes. Second, a foot of snow blanketed everything, including my car and the sidewalk leading to it.

Sighing, I retreated inside, pulled on some gloves and grabbed the battered snow shovel the Air Force had thoughtfully placed by each apartment door. I would become intimately acquainted with this implement during the next four years. After shoveling a path to my car and excavating it from its snowy grave, my shoes and pant cuffs were a soggy mess. The car groaned but finally started. I backed out, feeling the sweat from my shoveling labor dampen my undershirt. My good first impression was in jeopardy.

I cautiously guided the Ford Tempo over icy streets to the 321st Strategic Missile Wing's headquarters building, a four-story windowless box, about a mile away. I found an open parking space narrowed by a mountain of brown snow piled up on one side. Exiting the car with some difficulty because my door was partially blocked by the snow pile, I accidently caught my coat on the car's metal frame. Horrified, I watched as one of my three gold service coat buttons popped off. *Oh no. Not this. Not now.* I had ten minutes before I was due to meet my new commander.

There was no time to hire a seamstress. Wearing the coat with a missing button would be immediately noticeable and unacceptable. My other option was to ditch the coat and meet the commander in an alternative but proper uniform—dress shirt and tie. However, we were told to arrive in service dress. It is not a young lieutenant's dream to meet his commander while in violation of that commander's first directive. Yet, I really had no choice. I went with no jacket.

Upon arriving at the 447th Strategic Missile Squadron's third floor orderly room, I encountered two of my Vandenberg UMT classmates also assigned to this squadron. Their uniforms, of course, had the proper number of service coat buttons. As I began relating my tale of woe, I was notified that the commander was ready to see me in his office.

Lieutenant Colonel Rudy Meadows was a recruiting poster come to life. He was a tall regal man, wearing a perpetual look of cool confidence. Like his military record, the man's uniform was immaculate, covering what appeared to be a slender yet muscled frame. For a visual, think of a younger version of Gus Fring from the *Breaking Bad* television series.

He walked around his desk and welcomed me to the squadron with a crushing handshake and eyes giving me the once-over. He was smiling, but more in bemusement than warmth.

I was immediately intimidated and knew that he knew I was intimidated. I could see he had no problem with that. I introduced myself and quickly fumbled out an apology for being out of uniform because of an unavoidable button popping issue. "All right," was all he said, letting me guess what that meant, for good or ill.

He told me to sit which I did, waiting for him to sit first. With furrowed brow he began speaking about the importance of our nuclear deterrence mission, his hope that I would hit the ground running and many other important things which I didn't absorb because visions of buttons popping like champagne bottle corks were dancing in my head.

He then picked up my thin personnel record file from the desktop and read as I sat in awkward silence. One eyebrow raised. And not in a good way. He finally tossed the folder back down. The only thing he commented on was that I had received two speeding tickets the year before training. He wanted me to ensure that this "trend" didn't continue here. Launch crews drove government vehicles many miles to and from the launch control center sites every day.

I suppressed the urge to defend myself and say this was *not* a trend. I'd only received three tickets in my entire life. Besides, both of the ones in my record were the result of trying to keep up with the real reckless speeder, head basketball coach Steve Smith. He always drove the lead van on the Oak Hill basketball trips. I received both tickets after getting pulled over trying to catch up to him.

But an Air Force officer doesn't make excuses so I just swallowed and promised that it would never happen again. After receiving permission, I stood, saluted and left. I didn't know for sure but felt that if Lieutenant Colonel Meadows had a dog house, my name must now be Second Lieutenant Fido.

Thankfully, I soon settled into the initial work routine and put my introductory meeting behind me. Newbies from Vandenberg were not yet certified to pull strategic alert. We were first required to take several weeks of local training to learn how things operated at this particular base. So, it was back to the classroom.

Crew members weren't assigned offices, so during breaks from training at the headquarters building, we would just hang out in the mail room next to the squadron's front office. We passed the time by snacking and swapping funny Vandenberg stories. Occasionally, a veteran crew member would wander in and regale us with tales of alert life while he sipped his morning coffee. These accounts tended towards the weird, depressing and outright frightening. Kind of like older women telling their child-birth horror stories to expecting mothers. Scaring rookies has a long tradition.

The fun stopped, though, whenever Lieutenant Colonel Meadows happened to walk through the room, which was often. We were told that upon his entrance, we were to call the room to attention. So, a designated look-out would boom, "Room Ten-hut!" when he approached. We would jump to our feet and stand ram-rod straight until Lieutenant Colonel Meadows, feigning surprise, said, "As you were, gentlemen. As you were." We would then quietly take our seats, the conversation muted until he left the area.

Crew members from the other two squadrons told us they were directed not to call the room to attention when their commanders entered. Their leaders passed through these break rooms several times an hour and didn't want the troops popping up and down all day. Not our leader. He was an old-school Strategic Air Command guy. He wanted us on our toes at all times, never feeling comfortable in his presence. I assume he believed our fear of his response was part of what would motivate us to not let our guard down on alert. I guess that persona worked for him. Lieutenant Colonel Meadows retired many years later as a three-star general.

I was anxious to be done with local training and to start pulling my weight on alert. I was tired of studying although this period allowed us short workdays and more time to get our family settled. I was soon offered a three-bedroom house on base. It had beautiful wooden floors, a big yard dominated by a gigantic tree, a screened-in front porch and, best of all, a full basement that ran the length of the house. That space would become Brett's playroom on long winter days when he couldn't go outside. Just blocks away were the small base convenience store and the hospital. If snowed in, we could walk to either buy groceries or have our spleen removed. How convenient.

And the house was free. The Air Force didn't charge rent or ask tenants to pay for utilities or repairs. These and other military benefits made me feel valued, something I hadn't felt as keenly while teaching high school.

The next order of business was buying a second car. The Ford Tempo was not the vehicle of choice to make it through the snow and ice of a brutal northern winter. The crew veterans told the rookies that we needed to buy a "beater." These were older, bigger sedans whose heavy weight and thick metal frame between driver and outside objects was a priceless life insurance on slippery roads. Cars were beat up by the rough winter weather, so why take a nice vehicle out in the elements if you didn't have to?

Your beater was the Sherman tank you rolled to work and town in when Mother Nature turned nasty. No one paid much for a beater. The goal was to keep it running long enough to sell it to another new crew member when you left four years later. With the help of Mark, my car-loving father-in-law, I finally purchased mine. It was an old tan Ford Thunderbird.

In a previous life, it had served as an unmarked police car. You could tell by the twin search lights still affixed to the front windows. And the blood stains in the back seat. Only kidding. It cleaned up pretty good, but boy, was it a monster. You couldn't flip that thing with a bulldozer. Which was the idea. I was now ready for Old Man Winter to take his shot.

CHAPTER 14

Yes, But a Very Smart Monkey

"A monkey can do this job!" groused a missile crew commander as he stood next to me reading the monthly alert schedule. "Read a step. Do a step. Get a banana." I'd heard those exact words repeated many times by the veteran missileers I encountered during my initial weeks at Grand Forks. The sentiment perfectly encapsulated the typical missileer's rare blend of sarcasm and self-pity.

At first, I was offended to hear my newly acquired expertise disparaged in such a way. At the very least, I thought it should be conceded that a moderately intelligent monkey was required. Yet, I recalled that the nation's first astronauts were monkeys. So, Neil Armstrong and I had something in common. However, as local training wound to a close, my bigger concern was not whether a primate could do the job, but could I?

The morning of my first strategic alert, I donned the missileer's first line of defense—Air Force-issued long underwear. I then stepped into my crew bag uniform, a blue polyester version of the zip-up flight suit designed for pilots. Kind of like going to work in your pajamas. After lacing up my heavy black boots, I shrugged on a thick green parka in hopes of warding off what was forecast as below-zero temperatures.

I double-checked the A-3 bag I'd packed the night before. During winter months, I was required to bring my winter gear in case my crew partner and I were stranded on the road. My survival apparel included gloves with wool inserts, long wool socks, snow boots, sunglasses, a parka, long underwear and a ski cap. I was already wearing half of those items.

I ensured there was alert meal money in my wallet (yes) and that my prescription glass inserts were packed (check). The latter was needed in case of a capsule fire which would require my crew partner and me to don the bio-pack breathing apparatus. Last, I grabbed my technical orders case which contained three large checklist binders. My iron safe combination lock, possibly the most important alert item, was affixed to the case's handle.

Thus encumbered, I shuffled out to the garage and fired up the Ford

Thunderbird for a short drive over to the transportation building. I had grown somewhat accustomed to the cold, but this morning seemed especially miserable. I parked in the designated row reserved for crew deputies. Before abandoning my car to the elements, I pulled the cord protruding from the front grill and plugged it into the outlet in front of my parking space. The other end of the cord was connected to my engine block heater. Once plugged in, this block heater warmed the oil pan so my car would start when I returned the next day.

The man who invented the engine block heater in the 1940s was from, you guessed it, Grand Forks. Before this modern convenience, many North Dakota motorists would either pour hot water over their car's engine on winter mornings or drain the engine oil each evening before and take it into the warm house overnight.

Once my car was plugged in, I joined 14 other deputies for the glamorous duty of inspecting the Chevrolet Suburban government vehicles we drove out to the launch control facilities. Each vehicle was painted blue with clear *US Air Force* markings on the side. Not actually undercover transportation. In the vast winter whiteness of back-country North Dakota, these Suburbans stood out like big, blue, sore thumbs.

Sometimes I wondered if our vehicles might be attractive targets for an anti-nuke extremist hiding out in a roadside barn with a scoped rifle. The fact that this daily parade of ducks in a shooting gallery could travel unmolested via the public roads and small towns of North Dakota was a tribute to the law-abiding nature and patriotism of the local populace. If the nation's missile silos were located in Northern California, I imagined our daily commute would involve protester roadblocks, thrown rocks and other creative methods of harassment.

After completing our vehicle inspections, we all drove over to the wing headquarters building. The pre-departure briefing for all alert crews began at 8:30 a.m. in the third-floor conference room. That's where I found my commander, Jake Harvey.

I slid into the chair next to him and wished him a good morning. "We'll see," he replied. This would be my first alert, but number 168 for him. I had spent little time with Jake beyond my certification trainer rides. He struck me as a stand-up guy who knew his stuff but was weary of crew life.

"Here ya go, deputy," he said with a smirk, scooting over a small briefcase. "I guess we're bringing out classified today. Sorry, briefcase duty is a deputy-coded function." *Great. One more thing for me to lug around.* Most deputy responsibilities were outlined in formal regulations. Others however, fell into that catch-all category called, *whatever the crew commander doesn't feel like doing.* As they say in the military, "RHIP," or, "rank has its privileges."

New missileers at Grand Forks Air Force Base. At left is Mitch Catanzaro, the author's roommate at officer training. Author at right (courtesy Mitch Catanzaro).

The brief case was used to transport important papers. When it contained classified documents, that briefcase could never be out of the owner's possession. Yet humans are, well, human. Once, an absent-minded lieutenant accidently left his briefcase in a gas station where the crew had stopped on their way out to alert. I assume he'd been temporarily distracted by the purchase of a Big Gulp drink or box of donuts. The bigger gulp came for him when, one mile down the road, his crew partner asked him where the briefcase was. There followed several expletives, screeching brakes, flying gravel and a quick retracing of asphalt.

They arrived back at the gas station to find a nervous cashier pointing at the case, unmoved from its previous position on the floor. "I didn't touch it. I swear," she said with arms raised. Relieved, the crew grabbed the case and departed. Now there was a decision to make. Almost certainly, the briefcase hadn't been touched in the few minutes they'd been gone. It was also doubtful the cashier or the farmer sipping coffee out front intended to report them to the base. However, they were honor-bound to report themselves for a security violation. And so they did.

Admitting error is rarely rewarded in Strategic Air Command. I heard the offending crew received a Letter of Counseling in their personnel records and less than stellar annual officer performance reports. Pressured to take steps to ensure this violation never happened again, the wing leadership made a new policy. Missile crews were no longer allowed to stop anywhere on their way to, or from, alert. You need to go to the bathroom during your two-hour drive? Hold it. Want some donuts and coffee? Pack your own.

I jammed our briefcase between my feet and concentrated on the pre-departure briefing. It included a weather report, directions for filing the classified material in the capsule, a few general announcements and a review of security issues and missile maintenance activity in the field. I had prayed that my first alert would be a quiet one. Denied.

We were briefed that three of our flight's ten missile sites were undergoing major maintenance. That meant close coordination with the on-site maintainers and a litany of missile tests for us to run afterwards to ensure everything was accomplished correctly. And as if that wasn't enough, there was a command-wide communications exercise for all the capsules. Our communications-reporting performance would be graded and the results forwarded to the four-star Commander in Chief, Strategic Air Command (CINCSAC).

As unhappy as I was to hear this news, Jake was even more so. Since this was my first alert, he would shoulder most of the workload to keep us out of trouble.

After the briefing, we loaded our gear into the truck and headed out to Juliet-Zero, our home for the next 24 hours. Each launch control facility had a letter designation, spelled out in what's informally called the military alphabet. This is a method to speak letters, so they aren't misheard as other letters. So, instead of saying "J" over the radio, you would say "Juliet." That way, "J" isn't misheard as "K," for instance. The Juliet-Zero launch control facility was responsible for ten missile sites, labeled Juliet-01 through Juliet-10.

Unfamiliar with the local geography, I relied on Jake to direct me during the 90-minute drive down what appeared to be endless, identical country roads.

I would learn that these long commutes, while boring, were a good opportunity to get better acquainted with a crew partner. Although every crew member had an assigned partner, because of leave (vacation days), sickness, and other scheduling issues, a deputy could be paired with just about any crew commander on any given day. It was sometimes awkward to pull alert with a person you'd never met. Theoretically, if war broke out on your watch, he or she could be the person with whom you spent your final minutes on earth.

On many of these commutes, we would pass through a group of homes and businesses surrounding a single intersection. These sparse gatherings were somehow labeled as towns on our maps. One of these places was the subject of a missileer urban myth. Supposedly, although there were several trucks parked outside, no crew driving through had ever seen a living person. The legend was that the town was a North Dakota version of the one in the Stephen King novel, *Salem's Lot*. A town full of vampires who slept by day and prowled the prairie by night in search of human blood. Entertainment is cheap on a two-hour commute out to site.

As we drove, Jake reassured me about the busy alert ahead. "Don't worry about all the crap we have going on today. I won't go to bed until everything settles down."

"I appreciate that," I said, "but I'm sure I can handle most of it."

Jake nodded. "Probably so, but if something bad happens while I'm asleep, I'll get hammered too, because I'm the commander. Anyway, you can watch how I handle things and learn. Whatever happens, we'll be fine. Different day, same —. If we make it back home without launching a missile or breaking one, it'll be a success."

I asked him how he ended up in the missile career field.

"Well, I went to the Air Force Academy in Colorado Springs, which was sweet. I wanted to fly jets when I graduated, but my eyesight wasn't good enough to qualify. I thought missiles might not be too bad. It was still operations at least, and not some boring desk job. They sent me to Sicily to operate the Ground Launched Cruise Missile (GLCM) system. That was a great assignment. Took leave whenever I could. Traveled all over Europe, to France, Spain, Germany—you name it. The job was cool too. We were out in the field with the Army guys and our missiles were what made Russia think twice about invading Western Europe."

"So, what brought you to Grand Forks?" I asked.

Jake said that President Reagan's Intermediate-Range Nuclear Forces (INF) Treaty mandated that we pull our cruise missiles out of Europe beginning in 1988. So, Jake had to cross-train into another missile system. The Air Force assigned him to the Minuteman III. North Dakota was a let-down after three years in Europe.

Jake was from the upper Midwest and could take the cold, but after a while he was just sick of it. Even worse, there wasn't any action for single guys downtown. At least for Air Force guys. There were, however, plenty of pretty girls at the nearby university. He especially liked the beautiful Nor-wegian blondes who were plentiful in this part of the country. Unfortu-nately, most had little interest in dating "basers." They went for those local farm boys. He couldn't wait for his crew assignment to be over.

I felt bad for him. At least I had a wife and son to go home to. Although most crew members didn't enjoy North Dakota life, it was evident that the single officers were the most miserable group. When they gathered to socialize on the weekends, their shared misery was both a bond and an anchor.

Finally, Jake directed me off the main road and onto a small access road. It led up to a rectangular security fence which surrounded what looked like a large garage and a ranch style house with aluminum siding. This was the launch control facility. I stopped short of the fence while Jake radioed the flight security controller (FSC) inside the topside building which hosted the security team, a cook and an enlisted facility manager (FM).

The FSC answered and Jake responded with a call sign and code. It was correct so a young security forces airman trudged out to open the gate. "What happens if you accidently pass the wrong code word?" I asked.

Jake laughed. "That 19-year-old airman there would order us out of the truck, and make us lie face down in the snow. Then, he'd point that rifle at our backs while his buddy trotted out and verified our identity. The secu-rity troops get really bored on these three-day tours. They'd love nothing more than to place two officers face down in the snow." I made a mental note never to screw up the code.

I parked near the main building. We hauled out our gear and walked inside. To our right was the locked door to the security controller's room. The FSC let us in and then briefed us on the security status in the flight during the last 24 hours. Nothing unusual. He then picked up the phone and called down to the capsule crew. After Jake passed the crew a second

Oscar-Zero's topside support building, one of a dozen facilities at which I pulled alert. Behind the left corner window is where the security team monitored the front gate. The launch control center is directly below, six stories down (Library of Congress, HAER ND-12-A-1).

code, they buzzed open the door to the elevator shaft. We stepped inside and boarded an old utility elevator. I pulled the metal accordion door shut and pushed the *Down* button.

The elevator only stopped at one place and it was six floors below us. We descended to what, on paper, looked like a giant concrete barbell. The middle bar-like section was a tunnel junction at the bottom of the elevator shaft. On either end of the *barbell* were pill-shaped capsules, each the length of two school buses. The right-hand capsule was unoccupied and housed much of the launch control center's environmental control systems. The left-hand capsule was the control center itself. This is where the missile crews lived, worked and, if required, would launch up to ten intercontinental ballistic missiles.

When we arrived below, the deputy greeted us warmly as he slowly guided the four-foot thick, eight-ton blast door to its open position. This barrier served as protection both from a potential nearby nuclear detonation and from invading terrorists. Although weighing multiple tons, the massive blast door could actually be moved fairly easily. However, in training I had been cautioned that the blast door must be opened and closed slowly. Once it got up a good head of steam, it did not stop easily. "Bouncing the door"— allowing it to slam against the outside wall—could cause major damage. It could also damage a person's appendages. One deputy who lost control of the swinging door had instinctively stuck his foot out to block it from hitting the wall. The door slammed into his ankle, breaking it like a twig.

Entering the capsule was like entering a king's throne room. For some reason, the entrance was only about five feet high making all who entered bow deeply at the waist. Once inside the acoustical enclosure, the ceiling rose to a much more comfortable 15 feet. The floor was positioned half-way up the capsule, suspended from the ceiling by four giant shock isolators in each corner. This design was intended to allow the launch control center floor to give and gently rock while withstanding intense vibrations caused by a nearby nuclear detonation. The suspended floor consisted of metal plates covered by a rubber walking surface. As you walked, the floor bounced and swayed slightly beneath your feet.

Beneath the suspended floor, the bottom half of the capsule contained a row of large emergency batteries, survival gear and food, a motor generator, a sump pump, and in many cases, a few inches of standing water. Missile crews weren't allowed under the floor unless emergency maintenance was required. That was fine with me because who knew what slimy creatures inhabited that dark recess?

As we set our bags aside, the off-going crew commander gave us a brief wave, pre-occupied with some maintenance sergeant on the phone. The deputy was now hunched over his console, busy reading the printer which was expelling a continuous parade of missile status.

As trained, I fished out my crew change-over checklist. I expected us all to pause, circle up and make an orderly march through the checklist steps. Jake saw what I was doing and shook his head. "We need to get these guys out of here," he said. "I'll get the status from the captain when he's off the phone. You start inventorying the classified docs in the drawer." *What? This isn't how we did it at Vandenberg.* I had several questions for the deputy but he had now retreated to the bathroom to brush his teeth.

Reluctantly, I began inventorying the classified documents which on-coming crews were required to verify in case the off-going crew had either lost a document or was attempting to sneak one out. I noticed Jake now using his viewer to check all the seals on the crucial computer drawers to ensure they hadn't been tampered with. We were covering every required change-over step. Yet, we were doing them out of order and not as a crew as we had been trained to do. This didn't seem to concern anyone but me. None of the other guys even had the checklist open. I didn't like it, but, as the only rookie, kept my thoughts to myself.

"Locks," Jake yelled a few minutes later. The two off-going crew members removed their combination locks from the little red safe above the status console. This metal box contained the launch keys for the two consoles. Jake and I each secured our own locks in place of the ones removed. Now, the safe could not be opened by one person. Crew members were required to keep their lock combinations secret from each other. Jake and I signed for the alert, signifying that we knew what was going on and had verified that each crucial item was accounted for and configured properly.

The off-going crew wished us luck, grabbed our truck keys and hustled out of the capsule. Jake helped me close the blast door and latch it. All that remained was to hydraulically hand-pump the giant pins which slid out of the door and into open slots in the adjoining wall. Once completed, no one could open that door from the outside. It took 97 hand pumps to engage the pins. That was, of course, a deputy-coded function.

After pumping the door, I walked back into the capsule, my arm aching as if I had just pitched both games of a double-header. Things were chaotic with alarms going off, missile status lights blinking, prints printing and now Jake, like his predecessor, on the phone talking to a technician at one of our missile sites. I took a deep breath. Only 23 hours and 55 minutes to go.

Oscar-Zero launch control center entrance. Once the off-going crew departed, the large blast door would be shut and secured from inside the capsule (courtesy Peggy Weil).

CHAPTER 15

Sleeping on Alert

The next few hours were a blur of checklists, phone calls, alarms and a steady stream of prints generated by the multiple launch facilities with maintenance crews on site. The incessant alarms weren't necessarily a danger warning. They usually simply heralded the receipt of a test message or an expected missile status change. Alarms were more an assault on the ears than anything else. This morning, though, I was more irritated by how crew change-over had gone down.

It was clear that an actual alert would not play out like the ones simulated in training. I needed to adjust to that. Yet, I'd also need to draw the line when not following the checklist compromised security, safety or the mission. Nothing had risen to that level this morning. However, I was feeling the stress and information overload most would experience on their first day of a new job. I placed a large amount of trust in Jake, hoping that with over 160 alerts under his belt, he knew what he was doing.

My job now was to focus on the multiple tasks at hand—assisting maintenance teams at three of our launch facilities. To review, each launch control center had primary responsibility for ten missiles which were located at ten different launch facilities, geographically separated from the capsule and each other by several miles. The launch facility included everything above and below ground within its security fence. There wasn't much to see topside but a few sensors, antennas, an access hatch and a huge launcher closure door covering the top of the missile tube.

The critical components were all below ground. First, there was a large bi-level launch equipment room (LER) encircling the launch tube and housing power and air conditioning machinery, survival batteries and a huge ballistic gas generator. The latter was used to propel the enormous concrete launcher closure door down its rails clear of the launch tube opening so the missile could launch. Directly below this covering was the was the approximately 80-foot-deep launch tube which protected the six-story high Minuteman III missile.

These underground areas provided the only shelter on site. Above ground, maintenance workers were exposed to the elements. During the winter months, wind would whip across the barren site with no structures, walls or vegetation to shield a person from its bone-penetrating chill.

The launch facilities didn't have any surveillance cameras on site so capsule crews relied entirely on phoned in reports and control center print-outs to track what was going on during maintenance. That included the weather conditions. Maintenance troops prided themselves on toughing out the elements to finish their jobs. Yet, by mid-afternoon of my initial alert our last crew working had reached the breaking point. They phoned to report that the temperature was dropping rapidly, now approaching -60 degrees wind chill. To make matters worse, a snowstorm was slowly making its way across the prairie towards their location.

Jake agreed that the conditions were dangerous enough to call base and recommend that the team stop work and head home. This decision was not one to be made lightly. It meant the missile at that site would now remain off-alert overnight. Strategic Air Command prided itself on maintaining a high missile alert rate. So, any time a missile wasn't ready to launch, the explanation was scrutinized all the way up to the four-star commander.

Wisely, base leadership approved our request. We relayed the good news to the frozen workers who immediately began closing up for the night. One benefit of working in an underground capsule was being shielded from the weather 24/7.

With the last maintenance team on their way home, both Jake and I enjoyed a much-welcomed breather. There was still work to be done in the capsule though. We needed to check all the primary equipment racks to ensure they were in working order, test the communications equipment and send out computer reliability tests to all of our missiles. However, these once-every-24-hour requirements could now be accomplished at a more leisurely pace and without distraction.

Fortunately, we both weren't required to be awake for 24 hours. I learned that on a typical alert, there were few periods when either the deputy or commander was not asleep or lying down. This wasn't the case in the early years of missile alerts. The launch control center is considered a *No Lone Zone* meaning that one person can never be alone or unobserved while inside to prevent critical equipment from being secretly tampered with. To solve the crew rest issue, in the early days, there were three-person crews, allowing one person to sleep while the other two were up and within sight of each other. This set-up required a larger crew force which strained manning resources.

Eventually, the decision was made to put seals on the crucial equipment drawers, allowing one member of a two-person crew to sleep. When the crew member on rest status arose, he would check all the seals with a special lighted viewfinder to ensure they had not been compromised. If there were indications of tampering, the crew member discovering the problem would report the possible compromise to base leadership. The suspected crew member would be interrogated to determine if there was a reasonable explanation. If there wasn't, he or she would be immediately replaced with a back-up crew member. Then, the equipment would be thoroughly inspected while the investigation continued. I never heard of that happening at our base but I imagine it would be a tense atmosphere while the accused and accuser waited for the investigators to arrive.

The sleeping schedule was determined by each crew commander. Most would stay up with their deputies until after lunch. Since the afternoons were pretty busy with maintenance teams at the missile sites, this is when most commanders elected to take their sleep shift. They then would wake up around dinner, eat and let the deputy sleep from about 8:00 p.m. to 5:00 a.m. Then, the commander would roust the deputy once more to get another four hours of rest before the on-coming crew arrived. Most crew commanders felt that more sleep and a quiet shift was their reward for enduring two years of deputy duty themselves.

This alert had been too busy for Jake to take an afternoon sleep shift, so by 6:00 p.m. he was ready to hit the sack. Suddenly, for the first time, I sat alone at the console. Whatever happened, I'd have to handle it now. Despite his earlier assurances, Jake had called out from the bed in back, "Don't wake me up unless we're going to war or something's on fire." I wasn't sure if that was his way of showing confidence in me, or he was too tired to worry about my screwing up.

I now had time to contemplate the differences between a real launch control center and the simulated one in which I'd been trained. First, the real place smelled—and it wasn't the pleasing aroma of scented Christmas candles. This scent was a mixture of diesel fuel, brine and industrial chemicals with just a hint of human sweat. The latter wasn't surprising since this confined space had been continuously occupied by a parade of humanity for 25 years without undergoing, I presumed, a thorough cleaning. There wasn't maid service, so housekeeping was the responsibility of every officer who checked in for a 24-hour stay.

Whatever was wafting through that air, invaded the launch crew's clothes. The following day, most spouses greeted their returning missileer at the door with a demand to strip quickly. This had nothing to do with amorous desire but everything to do with expediting the cleansing of both their spouse and the offending clothes.

The capsule air was not only a little rank, but also freezing, due to the cooled air which was constantly piped through the rows of equipment racks.

The curtained bed in Oscar-Zero. Not Holiday Inn quality, but fine if you had a set of ear plugs. I slept there on many alerts (Library of Congress, HAER ND-12-B-16).

So, as soon as the off-going crew left, we shed our thin blue flight suits for warm cotton sweat clothes and tube socks. If a war broke out, this is the *uniform* all fashionable missileers would be wearing for World War III.

The capsule was also much louder than the trainer. Besides the constant drone of air conditioning, there was the added hum of electrical equipment and the whirl of the motor generator. Joining in with little harmony were the aforementioned alarms, ringing phones and printing printers. It felt more like I was inside a land-based submarine boring its way through the North Dakota dirt than a stationary capsule.

There were other more obvious differences from the trainer. We had a bed up against the back wall, enclosed on three sides with a curtain across the front to allow access. The curtains were heavy, blocking out all the outside light when pulled, but unfortunately, not all the noise. Many missileers wore ear plugs during their sleep shift, but I found the hum of equipment quite soothing as I drifted off to sleep.

Near the blast door was a small bathroom with a toilet and sink. No shower though. Also, in the back area, the Air Force had thoughtfully provided a mini-refrigerator and microwave oven. Nuclear war can really work up an appetite. These quality-of-life items were not part of our training equipment. Strategic Air Command was banking on the fact that we had mastered the art of sleeping, eating and operating a toilet without the aid of an air force checklist.

The capsule also came with more deadly equipment which hadn't been simulated in the trainer—our sidearms. Part of crew change-over was handing off two sidearms, each with ammunition and a holstered gun belt. These weapons were the military version of the Smith and Wesson, .38 caliber revolver. They only left the capsule once a year when they were switched out for new ones. During alert, the gun belts were usually hung on the blast door pump handle. This reminded us that we were required to wear our weapons every time this door was opened.

Sidearms were deemed necessary for the crew to defend the capsule against invading terrorists. You would assume that we were highly trained for this scenario. Not really. After initial qualification at the base firing range, we were only required to fire the handgun once a year to be re-certified. Beyond that, I don't remember being taught any shooting techniques or rules of engagement in case we were ever confronted with an intruder. In reality, there was probably a greater chance of us accidently shooting our own toes off, or each other, than of stopping Boris and his band of Russian paratroopers. As Jake observed, "If a squad of bad guys eliminates our six heavily armed security troops top-side and then somehow penetrates our massive blast door down here, how are we going to stop them?" The answer was—we weren't.

That said, I was proud of earning my small arms marksmanship ribbon in officer training. During that qualification session I had (according to official records) fired 36 rounds and hit my target 32 times. Not bad for a novice who had little experience with guns. If the capsule was ever attacked by stationary paper targets, I was going to do some damage!

Typically, the only outside people who ever observed me wearing a gun belt were the Air Force cooks who brought our meals down to the capsule. They didn't appear impressed. I guess my bed hair, Oak Hill Academy sweatshirt, pajama bottoms and fuzzy socks didn't conjure up an image of Dirty Harry. Just once though, I was tempted to greet them with my best Clint Eastwood imitation, "OK son, now very carefully, I want you to bend down and slide that bean burrito over to me, real slow-like. I'm a bit jumpy tonight so, like I said, make it slow."

Within that first year, an Air Force general made the decision to eliminate sidearms in the capsule. I don't remember why, but I imagine someone had said, "You know, it may not be a good idea to give two bored or possibly depressed missileers loaded weapons and 24 hours of isolation to ponder their life choices."

The alert evening activities increased when we were given a command-wide communications test. Capsule crews were tasked with ensuring all of their communications equipment were functioning properly beforehand so test messages could be received by multiple means. This redundancy was critical in a war environment when electronic magnetic pulse (EMP) waves from enemy bombs or other destructive actions might take out one or two types of communication methods that the command relied on to direct their missile crews.

One method command leadership used to communicate with the crew force during wartime was via radio from aircraft flying overhead. Missile crews were required to respond to their unique call sign at a moment's notice. Of course, during a wing-wide test, every other capsule was listening on the channel. This meant that if a crew member botched it, the whole world would know. No one wanted to be the only capsule crew in the wing that did not receive a test message because they had accidently misconfigured a crucial switch. That happened to one of my friends. Afterwards, whenever he would pass a group in the office hallway some prankster would mimic a radio voice and call out "Foxtrot-Zero? Foxtrot-Zero? Nothing heard. Break. Break." It was juvenile, but funny is funny.

Somehow, I made it through that initial test successfully without needing to wake Jake from his beauty sleep. I was proud of myself. I was finally getting this alert thing down. Or maybe not.

About 9:00 p.m., I was slumped at my console, exhausted from a full day and in danger of nodding off. Suddenly, there was a gigantic *boom* and the main lights went out. In my 21 years of active-duty service to the Air Force, I have never soiled myself. But in that moment, we almost had "clean-up on aisle two." My heart leaped out of my throat, hit the ceiling and then dived back down for cover. *What was that?!* There immediately followed what felt like a minor in-capsule tremor, then the emergency

Oscar-Zero control center viewed from the entrance, looking forward towards the status console. A small bathroom (no shower) and refrigerator are off camera, to the immediate right and left, respectively (Library of Congress, HAER ND-12-B-7).

lighting snapped on. I could hear the drone of equipment coming to life in the floor beneath me.

My first instinct was to wake Jake. Instead, I took a breath and quickly reviewed my training techniques. For unknown indications, I'd been taught to first scan nearby equipment racks for fault lights and also check for key problems like a lack of blowing air. As I did this, familiar signs began to pop up. Okay, this is what a power change-over is really like. I'd experienced these in the trainer but the simulation was not nearly as intense as the real thing.

Some outside condition had made the capsule lose commercial power. When that happened, computers reacted as if this was caused by a nearby bomb detonation. Outside air valves slammed shut, isolating the capsule from anticipated blast waves, radiation, etc.—thus the boom.

The capsule immediately lost primary lighting and switched to emergency battery power. Since batteries were limited in the breadth and duration of their equipment-powering capability, the diesel generator began to crank on. When ready, it would take over the capsule power load from the batteries until commercial power was restored. I had heard these change-overs were a common occurrence, especially during summer storms. I was not prepared for it in winter or for the more unsettling sounds associated with it. Soon, commercial power was restored and all was well. When I woke Jake up for his all-night shift, I was more than ready to hit the rack myself.

A few weeks after that alert, Jake and I were awarded Squadron Crew of the Month. Jake wasn't as excited about this recognition as I was. He said, "You never want to win this award. It usually means you had a lousy alert where a lot of bad stuff happened or someone got injured. Not happy memories." Our award write-up made a big deal of us recalling the maintenance crew because of frigid weather. You'd almost think Jake and I had trudged through the snow, found the guys passed out and carried them back to base on our backs where we resuscitated each one. The command was big on attention to detail when it came to work. But I was learning that a little hyperbole was greatly encouraged when it came to Air Force awards and commendations.

CHAPTER 16

The Missileer Code

Diversity was not the strength of the 321st Strategic Missile Wing's crew force. Approximately 90 percent of their numbers were male, most between 23 and 33 years of age, politically conservative and from lower-middle class to middle class backgrounds. They were also overwhelmingly Caucasian, although interestingly enough, my first two squadron commanders were Black. However, there was a small but vocal number of self-professed liberals sprinkled within the crews. The same could not be said for any gay missileers. I assume there were some. However, during my four years at Grand Forks, I never heard a single rumor about any officer being homosexual. Of course, admitting you were a homosexual in 1990 was grounds for dismissal from the service.

One important characteristic all 200 officers shared was competition for rank and recognition. Yet, as in any career where hard data is lacking, missileer reputations were built primarily on the twin pillars of personality and perception.

Facts are hard to come by in a missile wing where work is primarily accomplished behind secured doors, in windowless trainers or hidden below a North Dakota wheat field. Therefore, most of us had little direct knowledge of each other's job performance. As a deputy, the only crew members you observed on duty were the dozen or so commanders with whom you were assigned to pull alert.

Since most alerts were fairly uneventful, the best opportunity to observe a crew partner's performance under pressure was in the trainer. That interaction was even more exclusive, including no more than five or six people. A lieutenant had even less opportunities to observe his or her fellow deputies. Deputies were never paired with each other on alert or in the trainer.

So, most crew members' opinions of their peers were based on either random personal interactions or unreliable second-hand information. This situation tended to favor those who were socially adept and wore confidence as smartly as a well-pressed uniform. The culture was not as kind to those who, although often hard-working and bright, were the social equivalent of a wrinkled suit. As in many areas of life, style covered a multitude of deficiencies while the lack thereof tended to magnify them.

Once a crew member was subjectively assigned a place in the missileer hierarchy, it was hard to move up or down. A few early flubs and you were labeled "not very sharp." A few early successes paired with a winning personality and you were "going places in the Air Force." And per human nature, once people make a public assessment, they are loath to change it. Subsequent success by a bottom feeder is attributed to luck or a crew partner who "pulled them through that stellar evaluation." A golden boy's stumbles are attributed to bad luck or an incompetent crew partner who he could only save so many times in the trainer.

Unsurprisingly, some of the wing's shining stars didn't glow as bright when their Air Force career took them to new responsibilities. Conversely, many of those derided found great success after moving on from Grand Forks. Missile duty simply wasn't for everybody.

Early on in my assignment, I learned that the missile culture eventually sorted all crew members into one of four categories. The crew force facetiously labeled these as rock stars, shop weenies, line swine and slugs.

Rock stars were the exclusive club of half a dozen legendary missileers who appeared to sail through crew duty without stress or self-doubt. Each seemed to possess an almost divine understanding of the intricacies of the Minuteman III weapon system. They aced the three-monthly written tests while barely glancing at the material. They memorized dozens of checklists that the rest of us had to repeatedly reference. In the trainer, they were unflappable, often lecturing their humbled instructors on factual errors in the simulation scripts.

The rest of us wondered why these ten-ton brains had signed up for missile duty. Why weren't they out flying NASA space shuttles or discovering the cure for the cancer? The rock stars were revered, rarely challenged and allowed the social eccentricities that came with being one of the elite. They weren't universally loved, though. Humility was not their hallmark. They knew they were smarter than you and most of them couldn't be bothered to pretend otherwise.

A significant step below the rock stars were the shop weenies. They were characterized as having excellent job knowledge, high performance in the trainer and a solid work ethic. After serving 9–18 months as a new deputy or commander, these were the officers who were hired in the "shops." The shops were the instructor and evaluator offices. They offered weekday desk jobs to sharp missileers who in turn, created and provided crew force training and testing.

A shop position signified inclusion into the upper tier of the crew force. However, this group also had their detractors since they were only required to pull two alerts a month compared to everyone else's eight alerts. Rock stars, of course were also shop weenies and typically led these offices.

The line swine were the next level down on the hierarchy and, by far, the largest group. Despite their self-chosen nickname, they were generally well liked, solid officers who unfortunately were saddled with most of the workload. Typically, that meant pulling eight alerts a month. Many were, in my estimation, clearly instructor or evaluator material. Yet, for a variety of reasons, sometimes due to bad luck or personality, they had failed to distinguish themselves.

Without any shop time, the typical line missileer would finish their four years of crew duty with over 300 alerts. That's almost more time underground than a gopher. Unlike flying hours in the pilot world, in the missile culture, a high alert total was not a mark of distinction. Similar to golf, the missileer who finishes with the lowest alert total, wins. At least most line swine could take pride in the fact that, unlike slugs, they were still respected by their peers.

The slugs were a subset of the line swine. These were crew members who, although frequently sharp in other areas of life, had trouble meeting crew duty standards. Some studied hard but their personality type or mental wiring prevented them from doing well. Others had the potential to do well but were lazy and just didn't put in the work. The results were the same—poor performance and peers who did not want to be crewed with them, either on alert or in the trainer.

Like the rock stars, the slugs were an exclusive club of less than a dozen crew members. Few knew they were considered slugs because the term was primarily used behind their backs. Most were good people, but just not cut out to be missileers.

There was actually a fifth type of missileer. He or she could also be a member of any of the previous groups mentioned. They were informally labeled a part of the body that cushions you when seated. Like slugs, they were avoided, not due to their incompetence, but because of selfish ambition. Some would turn in their crippled grandmother for littering if it helped them get a shop job or win points with a high-ranking officer. Their common sins were blaming others for their own mistakes, never covering for a fellow crew member and spending much of their free time kissing up to the commander.

As over the top as these characterizations might seem, many in the crew force bought into them. To be fair, the accused often supplied ample evidence to support such perceptions. For instance, I remember one deputy who turned in his crew partner for driving ten miles per hour over the speed limit as they drove home from alert. Whatever minimal affirmation this might have brought him from the commander, it brought an even greater avalanche of derision from his peers. New crew members were often warned about these people the day they signed into the squadron.

This "cooperate and graduate" philosophy was just one way that missileers helped each other survive four years of crew duty. In addition, informal expectations were developed, disseminated and enforced for mutual benefit. These rules, like most social norms, were not written in any official document. However, they were verbally passed on from one generation of missileers to the next. To the wing veterans, a rookie missileer's naive enthusiasm and regulation rigidity presented a clear and present danger to the culture.

These informal rules were few, no more than three or four. Yet, within the crew force they were revered as if brought down from Mount Sinai by Moses himself. Baseball has dozens of unwritten rules such as never steal a base if your team is up by ten runs or don't flip your bat when you hit a home run. Violations usually result in a bench-clearing brawl. Missileers don't brawl. If these guys were fighters, they'd have joined the Marines. Yet, like the mean girls in junior high, they do get even.

Here are a couple examples of the Missileer Code.

1. *Thou Shalt Not Burn the Back-up:* This was a big one. No one enjoyed pulling their scheduled alerts. But everyone hated getting called in for alert duty during a scheduled day off. Each day, 15 missile wing crews were scheduled to go on alert. There were 15 wing launch control centers, each with two-person crews requiring relief every 24 hours. Sometimes, due to unforeseen circumstances, such as a pregnant wife going into labor, a bad injury or a death in the family, a scheduled crew member might need to be excused from alert duty at the last minute. Fine.

Each day there was a back-up deputy and commander scheduled. They were required to be at home, near the phone, so they could be quickly called in to replace a crew member. The back-ups though did not expect to be called in and they rarely were.

Injuries or a parent dying were one thing. However, if a scheduled crew member "burned the back-up" by calling in sick, well, he or she better be very, very ill. Like projectile-vomiting-every-ten-seconds sick, or baby-aliens-bursting-out-of-your-stomach sick. Better yet, they better be on the verge of expiring themselves, or already dead. Dead was an acceptable excuse. All other medical conditions were suspect.

He caught the flu? Tough. He has 24 hours to throw up in the capsule. That's why God invented toilets and trashcans. Communicable disease? She can avoid sitting near her crew partner on the drive out and change the sheets before sleep shift. About to die? Tell him to just lie down in the capsule and pass away. It's peaceful down there and he'll be buried underground anyway.

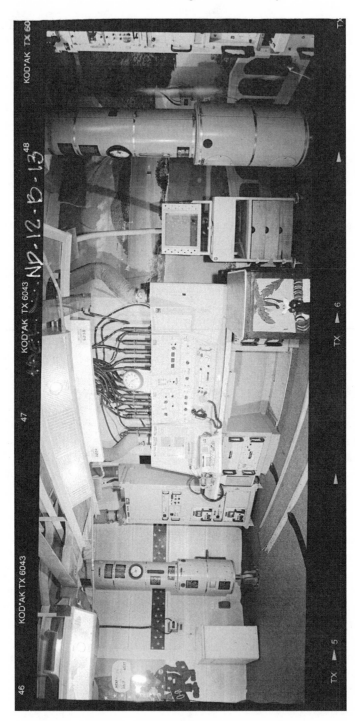

Oscar-Zero command console. Note two of the capsule's four large shock isolators on either side. They attached to the floor, suspending it from the ceiling. Their purpose was to cushion impacts from a nearby nuclear detonation (Library of Congress, HAER ND-12-B-13).

If you did transgress, word got around. "Hey, did you hear that Ron burned the back-up yesterday? I drove by his house in the afternoon and he was outside washing his car. The scumbag." If you did burn the back-up for sickness, it wasn't safe to show your face outside of the house for at least a couple days unless you were at the hospital emergency room.

2. *Thou Shalt Keep it in Family*: I never knew any crew member who did not take the mission, personnel safety or security, seriously. These were good officers, patriots and people who felt a deep responsibility to defend their country. Yet, we all worked under a back-breaking mountain of command rules and regulations, some of which made sense and others which seemed a bit excessive. As in many professions, workers soon determine which rules need to be followed to the letter and which may have some allowance for flexibility. Granted, one person's flexibility is another person's disturbing violation.

An analogy might be speed limits. Most would agree that driving well over the speed limit is often dangerous and puts the safety of passengers and other drivers at risk. It shouldn't be done. But if the speed limit is 65 mph, is driving 66 mph wrong or dangerous? Is 70 mph? Is 100 mph? All are technically against the law, but few would view them as the same level of recklessness.

One example: alarms in the capsule. Every time the capsule received a message, most of which were redundant test messages, the communications rack would light up, an irritating alarm would sound and the printer would loudly begin tapping out the message. This was easily heard throughout the capsule, even all the way back in the bathroom area.

Certain crew members hated these incessant alarms and reasoned that they could be temporarily eliminated with little risk. Seated at their console, they could easily see the communications equipment light up as well as hear and see the printer printing. Some crew commanders were reported to open up the communication racks and pull all the alarm power connections. Of course, this wasn't allowed. If an inspector or a squadron commander found out, both crew members would be in trouble.

A deputy crewed with a commander who liked to perform this kind of unauthorized sound pollution maintenance could either keep his mouth shut, report the commander to his superiors, or go to the commander, voice his displeasure and negotiate an arrangement. The latter path was an unwritten missileer rule. You both were adults—work it out. I knew fellow deputies who had an agreement like this with their commanders: I can't stop you from re-configuring some small stuff while I'm asleep, but (a) I don't want to know about it and (b) when I get up from my sleep shift you must have everything back the way it's supposed to be.

I'm not saying that was right, but that was one way it was often handled. If you turned a crew partner in for something that small, you better be ready for blow-back from your peers.

Yet, even a small deviation in procedures could result in unintended consequences. What if a deputy allowed his crew commander to disable an alarm and in mid-operation, the crew commander accidently broke off a more crucial piece of equipment? Now you've created a serious problem. And how would that be explained since there was no reason for a crew to even open that panel?

Another bone of contention could be the capsule's blast door. Unless the crew needed to let someone in or out, that door was required to be closed with the steel pins pumped into the wall recess (frequently taking 100 hand pumps). I heard of commanders who liked to just latch the blast door closed, but leave the pins unpumped. Their reasoning was that if the crew needed to harden the capsule during a war scenario or terrorist attack, there would be enough warning to quickly do so. Unpumped blast door pins was a bigger violation than alarm disabling. Almost all crew members would have an issue with the door not being pumped.

The only argument that made me somewhat sympathetic to just latching the door was fear of fire. If there was a fast-moving fire in the capsule, both crew members may only have a couple minutes to escape before passing out or being badly burned. Precious time could be lost if it took two minutes just to un-pump the blast door pins. No one wanted to contemplate being trapped in such a confined space during a fire. Yet, despite that fear, everyone I knew pumped the pins each time the blast door was opened and closed, which was typically four to five times an alert. I heard of commanders who refused to do it on their late-night shift, forcing any disapproving deputies to always perform the duty.

Integrity and professionalism are heralded concepts in the military. Yet, early on, young officers learn, in practice, those terms mean different things to different people. As Strategic Air Command officers, we were expected to follow directives to the letter. Achieving this high expectation was frequently tedious, laborious and contentious for our working relationships. We all had to navigate that sensitive area between meeting our own personal standards and working effectively with others who didn't share those standards. It wasn't easy, but it's a challenge everyone in every arena in life faces daily.

CHAPTER 17

How to Unbutton a Launch Silo

The Minuteman III missile's trigger is at the launch control center. The analogous gun barrel and bullet are five to ten miles away at the missile silo. The location of the silos, although not advertised by the Air Force, were public knowledge to the local populace. The silos and their above and below-ground support equipment were part of what was referred to as a launch facility. Most of these facilities were positioned right off public roads, carved out of a North Dakota farmer's field. The U.S. government compensated these landowners for allowing them to plant a weapon of mass destruction within spitting distance of their barns. A small payment, in my estimation, for turning the old homestead into a bull's eye target for a Soviet missile.

Each launch facility was surrounded by a security fence. There were no on-site security personnel to prevent a possible breach, nor even a video camera to monitor suspicious activity. There were, however, various sensors to detect and report any site penetration.

Back in the launch control center, these sensors triggered specific numbered printouts and two console lights. There was an outer zone light, or "OZ" which indicated movement inside the above-ground fence-line. The second light was for inner zone, or "IZ" and meant someone or something had at least begun opening the personnel access hatch to the underground launcher. It wasn't unusual to have an OZ light triggered during an alert.

A missile crew was expected to quickly react to any security lights by calling upstairs for a two-person armed response team to load up, jump in a truck and drive to the site to investigate.

Frequently, the response team discovered the perpetrator was a threatening rabbit who had burrowed under a security fence and was now scampering across the surface. Or, it might be a terroristic-minded tumbleweed rolling across the dirt. Once in a while, an actual homo sapien was discovered on site. These were typically the *protesteus erectus*, just arrived from Duluth Minnesota via a beat-up Volkswagen van to voice their displeasure with nuclear war. Well-meaning but harmless, these pacifists would climb the fence and be observed by the response team chanting peace slogans while sprinkling blood around the edge of the silo. One time, a more industrious protester was found standing on top of the launcher closure door, unsuccessfully attempting to batter a hole in it with a sledgehammer. The difficulty of accessing the underground launcher was one reason there was no need to post armed security guards at these sites.

For the bored security responders, spending their third day out in the field, encountering a real live protester was a welcome break from the tedium. It was also a rare chance to practice their takedown skills. Regretfully for training purposes, few of these gate-crashers were interested in resisting a couple of teen-agers with automatic rifles. Most protesters gladly surrendered. Frequently, they would happily chat up their captors while all waited for the local county sheriff to arrive and take them into custody.

The launch facility visitors with official government business were usually our missile wing maintenance teams. They performed tasks which ranged from scheduled annual equipment upkeep, to troubleshooting missile computer problems, to the ultimate task—placing a new missile into the launch tube and bringing it up on alert. The alert status of a missile was crucial. Strategic Air Command was proud of maintaining a missile alert rate above 95 percent. That far exceeded the alert rate of both our fighters and bombers, a rare bragging point for the missileer community versus the flying world.

So, there was immense pressure on launch crews not to do anything that might, even for a few hours, take a missile off alert status. Even more so, maintenance crews felt pressure to fix an off-alert missile in their daily allotted hours. For safety reasons, they were limited to working a 16-hour day before a required eight-hour rest break kicked in. That would seem like plenty of time to complete a job. However, those 16 hours also includes what could be up to four hours of commute time between base and the work site. In addition, once a maintenance team reached the launch facility, it often took an hour to gain access to the underground areas and set up work equipment.

At the end of the day, reversing those actions and securing the site was also time-consuming. So, only about half of a workday would involve actual hands-on maintenance of the missile. As the day wound down, with the clock ticking towards that limit, the maintenance crew and launch control crew needed to work closely to bring the missile up on alert. If they didn't succeed, it meant an additional 10 or 12-hour delay before that missile's target was covered again.

On any alert, a missile crew could be working with maintenance teams at multiple missile sites in their flight. When a maintenance team arrived at the launch facility, communication was set up between the team, capsule crew and the capsule crew's above ground security controller. The maintenance team chief would pass a code to the missile crew to prove his identity (remember, no cameras) and to also ensure he wasn't under duress by a bad guy. Once the code was verified, the maintenance team was allowed to proceed on site. From that point, the outer zone, and eventually the inner zone security light, would illuminate at the control center status console and remain on.

It took a while for maintenance crews to access the underground launcher. Their first barrier consisted of two combinations that needed to be inserted for the personnel hatch to unlock. The maintenance team chief is passed one combination by the capsule crew and our topside flight security controller passes the other combination to the on-site security team chief. As with many aspects of nuclear weapons it takes two authenticated individuals to gain access to a physical area or crucial equipment.

Once the maintenance chief and the security team chief inserted their individual combinations, the access hatch could be opened. At this point a mechanism was activated which lowered the concrete plug blocking the hatch. After the plug reached the bottom, a person could climb all the way down the ladder into the launcher area.

The descending plug was on a very slow timer, set for various minutes depending on the distance between the launch facility and the owning launch control facility where the armed response team was stationed. The concept was that if a bad guy somehow obtained the two codes to access the missile, the slow descending plug would give the capsule crew time to detect the unauthorized access lights illuminating, call a security situation and have the response team arrive at the launch facility to intervene.

The only other way to get at the missile was through the 110-ton, concrete launcher closure door which covered the launch tube. That was next to impossible.

Once the maintenance team climbed down the access hatch ladder, they were positioned on the top level of a two-level launch equipment room. This was a ring of computer and monitoring equipment racks which encircled the upper outside wall of the launch tube. Within the steel and concrete walls of the launch tube was the Minuteman III missile, poised to fly within minutes of a launch command.

The missile itself is three stages of solid propellant, almost sixty feet long with a 5.5-foot diameter, leaving little launch tube workspace for technicians. Sitting in the shroud atop the missile are up to three re-entry vehicles, all nuclear weapon-capable and able to hit separate targets. The Minuteman weighs almost 80,000 pounds and its first stage can generate over 200,000 pounds of thrust, propelling its payload northward approximately 6,000 miles.

One reason that some of the more southern states, like Georgia, were originally considered, but not selected to host missile sites was that the Minuteman couldn't reach Russia from that distance. Another factor was that a southern state siting meant a longer ballistic trajectory over the United States. Apparently, we weren't as concerned about over-flying Canada.

For the missile maintenance technicians, the primary concern is getting the day's job done. An opening in the launch tube wall allowed them to walk a short gang-plank-style platform and access the upper portion of the missile. Beneath the gang plank was a several-story drop to a concrete floor. The missile itself was elevated off the floor of the launch tube by a shock-absorbing hydraulic system.

Maintenance technicians also needed to access areas off the gang plank, both around the side of the missile and down below. For those tasks they hung what was called a work cage. Similar to what you might see utility workers ride in while working up on telephone poles, the small bucket was only big enough for two people at a time. Its mount and motor hung from a metal ring affixed near the top of the launch tube. The ring allowed the work cage to travel horizontally around the missile. Heavy cables allowed it move up and down the side.

Like a launch control center, the entire underground launcher area was a No Lone Zone. Whether required or not for the work project, two people had to always be in sight of each other while within the confines. This was a safeguard against tampering of critical equipment. Although required for security, such restrictions could slow down maintenance.

Ironically, most missile launch officers never set foot in a launcher, or laid eyes on the actual missiles they were certified to launch. Other than training enrichment, there was no reason for a launch officer to visit a launch facility. Another missileer and I were lucky enough to be given one such opportunity during our first weeks on crew. On a training day, our instructor drove us out to a site so we could observe some missile maintenance. We were even given a ride in the work cage.

It's sobering to be able to reach out and touch a live missile, primed to destroy people and property. I kept wondering how fast we could get out of there if the klaxon rang and we realized that monster was being directed to launch. Talk about an adrenaline rush!

One event I never witnessed, but would have liked to, was a missile emplacement. For that delicate operation, Minuteman IIIs are driven out to site in a transporter erector loader (TEL) with convoy escort. The TEL is an approximately 65 foot-long, low-slung, semi-looking truck. As you might imagine, it is driven very slowly out to site, never topping 30 mph and frequently moving at a crawl. It's accompanied by a bevy of officials, armored security trucks and many prayers—especially by the driver. Although the state's weather conditions can be brutal, eastern North Dakota roads are typically straight with little traffic and almost no hills. Even so, attempting a hairpin turn onto an access road with sixty feet of truck bed behind you is somewhat stressful for a young driver.

If a turning maneuver goes bad and the truck starts to tip off the road, about a dozen people, including each of their supervisors, see not only the truck teetering on the edge, but also their careers. In the military, and especially in our command, if a lowly sergeant screws up, they aren't the only one facing punishment. Often, the direct supervisor, the supervisor's boss and the supervisor's boss's boss are also in line for reprimands and possibly firing. Strategic Air Command's viewpoint was that if Sergeant Snuffy messed up it must mean that his supervisor didn't train him properly. The supervisor's boss and his boss are also to blame for accepting working environments where young sergeants are not trained properly and allowed to be incompetent.

My first year at Grand Forks a missile convoy was cautiously rolling out to a site when this very scenario occurred. The TEL driver pulled too tight a turn. To his horror, the truck's left-side wheels slid off the road into a ditch. The truck leaned over and appeared to be in danger of rolling upside down. Miraculously, it held fast. Heavy equipment was quickly called in to right the truck. The delicate missile being transported didn't sustain any significant damage.

The next day, our wing commander briefed the out-going alert crews on the incident. He said, "The only thing keeping that truck bed from rolling over was my ass." How true. If it had rolled, he might very well have been fired. But it didn't and he went on to become a four-star general, ultimately commanding all the space and missile forces in the United States Air Force. Nice recovery.

Once on site, the TEL was backed over the open launch tube with the closure door pulled aside. Then, giant hydraulic actuators raised the missile container to a horizontal position over the hole. After being properly aligned, the missile was slowly lowered down into the launcher via a winch. Once in place and secured, it was then ready to be mated with the shroud containing the re-entry vehicles. If you're wondering why the weapons weren't already attached to the top of the missile before transport, I refer you to my story above. The only thing worse than a missile crushed in a ditch is a missile with nukes on it, crushed in a ditch.

If a maintenance crew was unable to finish their assigned task with enough time on the clock to drive back to base, they were forced to RON, or "remain overnight" in bedrooms at the nearby launch control facility. Since those accommodations are a step below a Fargo, North Dakota, Motel 6, maintenance crews were motivated to get their work done and head home. However, work on a strategic missile is critical, deliberate and by the book, with little opportunity for cutting corners. For good reason.

Wyoming underground launcher with Minuteman III missile. Note the missile maintenance technicians in the work cage, which moved both vertically and horizontally to access key compartments of the missile (U.S. Air Force).

In 1980, two airmen from a propellant transfer team were working in an Arkansas ICBM silo, checking oxidizer tank pressure on a Titan II missile. To expedite their final task, they decided to use a new ratchet, readily available and approved for some procedures, but not for their particular job. The substitute tool did not fit as snug on the socket. To their horror, in the middle of a turn, the socket slipped off the ratchet. Before they could catch it, the socket fell 80 feet, bounced off of a thrust mount and pierced the skin on the missile's liquid fuel tank. The leak began a series of catastrophic events which ultimately culminated in a missile explosion and the loss of an airman's life.

Fortunately, the Minuteman IIIs at Grand Forks were designed with solid propellant which is much less volatile than the Titan II's liquid fuel. Even so, there is always significant danger if maintenance crews do not follow their technical procedures. During my crew tour we were briefed about a sad example of one such mistake. A missile maintenance team was reaching the end of their authorized workday and were anxious to pack up and hit the road. They had just disassembled the work cage and were carrying it out when one of the airmen noticed they had not properly secured an access point on the missile. The location was too far below the equipment room deck to reach by hand. The work cage would need to be reassembled, hung, and then used to reach and secure the access point. That would add 30–45 minutes to their day and possibly force them to stay overnight in the field.

One technician had the dubious idea that since the access point was not that far down, he could, using his coworkers as anchors, rappel the few feet down the launch tube wall holding on to a fire hose.

Putting the unauthorized plan into motion, the volunteer walked himself down and secured the port. Unfortunately, he found waning strength and sweaty hands made the climb back up more difficult than anticipated. Before his coworkers could reach him, he slipped off of the hose and fell 40 feet to the bottom of the launch tube, hitting the concrete floor and severely injuring himself.

His panicked colleagues could hear his anguished cries, but couldn't reach him without the laborious and time-consuming task of installing the work cage. Even then, they were essentially helpless to assist the injured colleague until the emergency medical response team arrived. This took what seemed like an agonizingly long time due to the missile site's isolated location. I understand the young man survived, but I'm not sure in what condition.

For many of these accidents and other sensitive incidents, information was sketchy and frequently arrived third-hand. The Air Force was not in the habit of sharing embarrassing events with the media, the public or even their own troops, unless absolutely necessary. As a result, for most missileers, it was difficult to verify the facts and sequence of events for any incident they were not a direct participant. In one sense, that's understandable. Some of the incidents involved classified information. Yet, even for those that did not, the Air Force was reluctant to alarm the public, lower the morale of its personnel or give ammo to their critics and enemies.

Chapter 18

Women in the Man Cave

The Bible states that before God created Eve, he observed Adam and noted, "it is not good for the man to be alone." In the early Strategic Air Command translation, there is an added phrase—"except in a launch control center."

When I began crew duty in 1989, the missile wing at Grand Forks had been operating for almost 25 years. Yet, female crew members had only been a part of the organization for just over 12 months. In every military branch, women were slowly making in-roads to operations-related jobs which had historically been open exclusively to men. Most airmen saw this expansion as progress. Others viewed it as an unwelcome invasion.

There was little doubt that women could perform crew duty as well as any man. The greater concern among the crew force was that the influx of women would change their culture, social rules and male camaraderie. I do believe that in the process of gender integration, some good things were lost. Yet, much of the antiquated and crude "frat boy" behavior was jettisoned also. *Good riddance*, I thought. Gender integration was needed and overdue.

One might assume that the harshest critics of mixed-gender crews were the male missileers. However, an almost bigger outcry came from their girlfriends and wives. Many weren't happy with the prospect of their men spending an isolated 24 hours with a female. Hormones being what they are, they feared a capsule offering a bed and zero chance for observation provided potential temptation.

Air Force leadership anticipated the initial resistance gender-mixed crews would create. However, they also knew that the days of excluding women from operations jobs were numbered. These positions clearly provided a promotional and military awards advantage to those who occupied them. Counterarguments about the risks to unit cohesion and discipline, not without some merit, were not strong enough to carry the day.

In the early 1980s, to make the integration of female crew members more palatable, the Air Force began placing all-female crews at a couple of missile bases. This temporarily avoided pairing males and females.

Unfortunately, it also put an added strain on the female crew members. If any women needed to miss an alert because of sickness, injury or a medical condition, she had to be back-filled by another female. There weren't enough female crew members at the wings to make this work. So, at times male crews had to fill in, even if only one female in a crew couldn't work. This exacerbated the resentment from the males. It was clear that gender-based crews were not a long-term solution.

When I arrived at Grand Forks, less than a dozen of the almost 200 crew members were female. Increased scrutiny of this small group brought additional pressure for them to perform at a high level. Despite the spotlight, all the female crew members I worked with were professional, personable and wanted no special treatment.

The women married to other crew members seemed to assimilate easier. The single females had to walk a much finer line to gain acceptance. If overly feminine or attractive, they faced criticism for either being flirty or using their looks to gain favor. If they intentionally downplayed their femininity, they were often viewed as "trying to be like a guy" or "overcompensating."

Despite their professionalism, these were still young women in their twenties who were interested in dating and having an active social life. Since the Grand Forks civilian community did not fully embrace the military, few of my fellow crew members, male or female, appeared to have many friends from town. As officers, they were not allowed to date enlisted personnel or anyone above or below them in their chain of command. That left the primary dating pool to fellow junior military officers. Yet, mixing work and relationships was a delicate balance.

A few of the females seemed to revel in the 20–1 ratio of men to women. Some were no doubt receiving more male attention than they had ever experienced. The downside was that a few were faced with frequently repelling well-meaning, but unwanted, interest from co-workers. This was a delicate operation, since a rebuffed suitor might retaliate by disparaging the young lady to other crew members.

Most of the men, though, weren't interested in a work-related romance. They had no trouble in acting professional around their female counterparts. And even if they were tempted to behave boorishly, their bad impulses were kept in check by fear of a career-impacting perception.

Although never a concern of mine, some men feared that a false sexual harassment claim might be leveled against them. With no cameras or listening devices in a launch control center, any below-ground accusation came down to a he-said, she-said. The paranoid fear was that a female might make an accusation either as revenge for a perceived slight or as a way of forcing a transfer out of missiles.

I learned how real this concern was one evening before an alert when my phone rang. It was a crew member from another squadron whom I didn't know well. He was scheduled to pull alert the next day with a new female missileer, not his regular partner. He asked if I'd be willing to switch deputies with him.

According to him, he was asking because she had recently accused one of his buddies of sexual harassment. His friend had been assigned as her new assignment sponsor. This was a typical duty tasked to a unit veteran to help a newcomer with in-processing and finding housing. The caller claimed that while performing normal sponsor duties, his friend thought he perceived a mutual attraction with this new lady. After a few days, he asked her out. She turned him down and then interpreted his subsequent behavior as continuing to pursue her. Eventually, she complained to squadron leadership. Now the rumor had spread that she was imagining everyone wanted to date her.

I didn't necessarily buy this story but agreed to switch. In retrospect, I'm surprised that the scheduler allowed us to do so. It seems like a bad precedent to set. I pulled 240 alerts in four years and this was the only time I was ever asked to switch crew partners.

The next morning, as I waited for this young lady at pre-departure, I began to have second thoughts. Was I setting myself up for an unwarranted charge? What was she going to be like? Would I need to watch my every word and action for the next 24 hours?

My worries turned out be unfounded. She was very nice, although somewhat reserved. Nothing about her struck me as delusional or having the demeanor of a man-hater. I concluded that her male sponsor very likely had gone over the line. Sadly, now added to the pressure of learning a new job, she had to deal with unfair perceptions and possible ostracization within her squadron.

I soon learned that the female crew members, although sharing gender, were quite diverse in both temperament and personality. Most were smart and goal-oriented. Several were selected as instructors or evaluators. A couple of them though, earned a reputation for being somewhat scatter-brained. In other words, unsurprisingly, female crew members ran the gamut, just like their male counterparts.

One of the female crew members I knew fairly well was married to a guy in my squadron. They had dated during Vandenberg training and married before moving out to Grand Forks. She was tall, attractive, and excelled both as an athlete and as a missileer. Like me, her sport was basketball, which she had played in college. We both made the base varsity teams one season and the next year played on the same wing intramural over-30 team. She was the only female in the league, but was far from a novelty act. She scored 32 points in one game, the highest total of anyone that season. Later that year, she was chosen for the All-Air Force team.

Despite the significant cultural change of bringing females into the crew force, I can't recall any formal training or squadron discussions on that subject. Our leadership never addressed what was considered appropriate or non-appropriate behavior in a mixed-gender environment. That seems odd in a command that had a checklist for answering the capsule telephone and mandated pre-softball-game safety briefings on watching out for slippery grass. Maybe they assumed we already knew how to conduct ourselves.

It was true that we had previously been in mixed gender environments during officer training. Yet, even there, I don't recall the subject of male-female boundaries being discussed beyond the prohibition of dating either enlisted personnel or your boss.

This neglect changed dramatically in 1991 after the Navy Tailhook Association scandal rocked the military. During that annual convention of Navy fliers, several female military members complained of being groped in the hallways by drunken males while walking the gauntlet from the elevator to their rooms. Congress and the Navy investigated, pulling back the curtain on a locker-room culture that had ignored this and other boorish behavior for years. One admiral even compared the female complainers to "whores" and worse. He was quickly fired from his command position along with many others. The riot act was read throughout the Navy and the other services. Sexist and harassing behavior would no longer be tolerated.

It was soon after this scandal that the Air Force instituted annual sexual harassment training. A new term was introduced—"a hostile working environment." We were trained that such an environment was created not only by sexual comments to, and unwanted touching of, co-workers, but also by less obvious (to some) actions. Telling crude jokes in the workplace, even with no females present, was no longer tolerated. I thought of one of my Vandenberg instructors who on the first day of training threw a cartoon up on the overhead projector. It depicted male and female genitalia with legs running. I won't share the caption. Anyway, now just a few years later, he would be immediately fired for such behavior.

Eventually, displaying any signs or pictures which could be construed as suggestive or sexual in nature was prohibited. For some, this was a shock. Yet, I'm proud to say that for the vast majority of crew members, these guidelines only reinforced the professional behavior they already exhibited.

In 1991 I observed the first of what would be many purges over the years of inappropriate displays in the workplace. Although I never saw any pin-up girls or sexual content displayed in office areas, several capsules had PG-rated Nordic art figures painted on the walls or ceilings of the launch capsules. The Mighty Thor with his loin cloth and hammer were acceptable. But the Warrior Princess and her plunging neckline and leather miniskirt were painted over.

Several years later, a decree came down from Air Force headquarters that each squadron commander was required to inspect every office and workspace under his or her command for inappropriate displays. The poor civil engineer commander I worked for at the time had over 400 people and 20 buildings to inspect, room by room. During my instructor days at Vandenberg one such purge required a co-worker to take down from his cubicle a glamorous but wholesome picture of singer Shania Twain. Even some photos of wives and girlfriends were deemed too risqué.

By the last years of my Air Force career, sexual harassment/assault training was as common as security and leadership training. Each wing had a full time Sexual Assault Response Coordinator (SARC), volunteer victim advocates, new rules which provided reporting victims confidentiality and zero tolerance for any unwanted behavior, displays or comments.

This was not the case during my Grand Forks assignment. Yet, I recall only one significant sexual misconduct allegation. Without going into detail, assertions were made that several crew members had engaged in consensual sexual activity while on alert. Some of those identified married to other people which made it even worse. Most alarming though, was subsequent word that one crew member had been accused of sexual assault.

Our wing leadership did not share any of this information. It was leaked by a few crew members who claimed first-hand sources. Either they had talked to one of those involved or played some role in the internal investigation.

Rumors began flying like Minuteman IIIs after a launch order. Facts were few. Opinions were bountiful. *There are predators among us that need to be expelled! No, it's all a lie to get back at certain people. I believe it was consensual, but now the person is embellishing the facts to excuse their poor job performance.* Of course, the only people who knew what actually happened were the accuser and the accused. I wasn't close friends with any of them, so remained in the dark like everyone else.

Despite the leaks, our leadership did their best to keep a lid on information. That's understandable. Preserving the integrity of an investigation and the privacy of those involved is crucial.

As I recall, within a few weeks, a couple people were quietly re-assigned and that was that. No announcement of investigation findings, charges filed, or punishments rendered. Not even an informal acknowledgment of the accusations. Maybe there simply wasn't enough evidence to justify briefing the crew force.

What I do remember is unexpectedly encountering one of those

Lima-Zero crew member artwork on launch control center wall above inside entrance. You can also see names written on the side wall. Tradition called for crew members pulling their last alert to sign the wall. (Library of Congress, HAER ND-13-P-1).

involved at the base library. Unbelievably, the person had been temporarily assigned duty at the check-out counter. The Air Force version of a Time Out. I thought it an odd decision to place them at such a public location. Was that for their own protection or to embarrass them further? I know it made for the most awkward book-stamping experience of my life.

Soon after my library encounter, the book-stamper was gone from the base. Where that person ended up, I don't know. For us, it was back to work as if nothing had happened.

Unprofessional behavior on alert was rare, but not unheard of. Once, a co-worker of mine rode out to alert with a deputy he'd never been paired with. As they approached the control center site, the deputy asked if it was all right for him to bring some beer on alert. Shocked, my friend told him if he had any, he'd better dump it out before they arrived at the security gate. No alcohol was allowed on site, period. The deputy then laughed and said, "I was only kidding. I didn't bring any."

Later that night, after the deputy had gone to bed, my friend wandered back to the little capsule refrigerator and found a milk jug filled with yellowish liquid. He opened the top, sniffed, and sure enough, it was beer. Now angry at the position his crew partner had put them both in, he did the right thing. He immediately notified the topside security controller and the base command post of what he'd discovered. Base leadership immediately called in the back-up deputy and flew him by helicopter out to the site.

When my buddy woke up the deputy and let him know what was happening, the guy tried to grab the jug and dump the beer down the toilet. By then, one of the security controllers had entered the capsule and prevented him from doing away with the evidence. After being flown back to base, this dumb young man was immediately decertified and never pulled alert again. Bizarre.

What this all taught me was that you can investigate people's backgrounds, give them psychological tests and set up strict rules, but in the end, you are dealing with human beings. You never know what they might do.

CHAPTER 19

Why So Testy?

In 2015, missileers received the most media attention they'd had in years. The story was covered by national television as well as major newspapers such as *The Washington Post* and *The New York Times*. To the embarrassment of the Air Force, the focus was on a scandal.

Over 70 missileers at Malmstrom Air Force Base in Montana were implicated in a cheating ring. A base investigation had uncovered the wide-spread sharing of monthly test answers via social media. The scandal was shocking to a general public who admired the Air Force for its three core values: integrity first, service before self, and excellence in all we do. As a former missileer, I was disappointed by the news, but not surprised.

From the early days of Strategic Air Command, written tests were a major tool used to evaluate those responsible for employing nuclear weapons. Although monthly simulator sessions were more indicative of a missileer's competence, trainer rides were a cooperative endeavor. A poor crew member could still pass a trainer ride by leaning on a strong partner. In a written test, each officer was on his or her own.

There were three written tests administered each month—36 a year. In a career field with few real-world trials to distinguish one crew member from another, monthly test scores became an easy tool in ranking officers. Although having little correlation to a crew member's competence on alert, test scores took on an inflated importance. They were cited in wing awards and annual performance reports, and used as yardsticks in hiring for coveted wing positions. As with trainer evaluations, a failing grade meant decertification.

This created anxiety among a young crew force, where all were competing for recognition and a sterling record. Unsurprisingly, even for officers who prided themselves on professionalism and honor, there was a temptation to cheat.

Exacerbating this issue was the very slim margin for error. For the monthly Emergency War Order (EWO) test, the passing grade was 90 percent even though the expectation was that the crew member would score

100 percent. Missing a question from time to time was forgiven, as long as you kept your average above 95 percent. Any average below that, especially in the 90–92 percent range, marked you as a poor performer.

The other two monthly tests were weapons system and codes control. The passing score for them was only 80 percent. They were taken on the same training day, called T3/4. Both were open book if you brought your technical orders. Weapon system training was taught, and the test administered by your peers. These were shop guys who still pulled alerts each month like everyone else. Senior leadership did not give weapon system test scores the same level of scrutiny as EWO scores.

If T3/4 felt more like a college quiz atmosphere, EWO, called T1, felt like a final exam in that one class you were barely passing. T1 was taught by senior captains who had already completed their crew tours. They were sympathetic to our plight but were not our buddies like the T3 instructors.

Mercifully, all formal Air Force tests are primarily multiple choice with possibly a fill-in-the-blank or two. There are no long essay questions like "Describe in depth, using real-world examples, the unit morale and individual emotional implications of pilots getting all the women."

With a typical EWO test consisting of 30 questions and an hour to finish, excellent test-taking skills and a logical mind were crucial. The only test aid allowed was a list of missiles you could mark to keep track of which ones had launched in the scenario and which remained.

Crew partners took T1 and T3/4 sessions together so they could discuss procedures during the training portion. But once the test was administered, no communication was allowed.

Questions could be tricky: Was the launch message in the scenario decodable enough to act on it? Does this message direct configuring missile X for launch but not missile Y? Was it all of the above? None of the above? Do you need help from Heaven above? Yes, please.

When stuck on a question, a test-taker had three choices—guess, walk up and ask the instructor for clarification, or cheat. Many chose to join a long blue line of befuddled crew members waiting to ask the instructor a question. Instructors were only allowed to clarify a test question, not give hints. However, some crew members were masters at pushing that boundary. They would continue to poke and reword their question until a worn-out instructor either slipped and offered a key nugget of information or banished them to their seat.

Other test-takers, lacking such prosecutorial talents, either guessed or possibly cheated. Although my sense was that cheating was rare, I know it happened. In the pre-cell phone and internet days, the methods were traditional—either looking over a nearby shoulder or, more daring, secreting a list of answers given to you by a buddy who had taken T1 earlier in the month.

The T1 instructors, all former crew members, were not dumb. They hawked the test room, but were often distracted by the long line of missileers waiting for clarification. Their second line of defense was to create multiple test versions. This helped, but most cheaters recognized a question even if it was reworded or renumbered.

For the record, I never cheated on an EWO test. Not that I wasn't tempted. One of my first annual performance reports stated that I had gone the entire year without missing a single EWO question. I lay that to good test-taking techniques rather than mastery of EWO. Which makes my earlier point.

I would not have been a successful cheater anyway. Case in point: seventh grade in Hawaii. It was music class, certainly not my best subject. We were given what I thought was a particularly unfair test and I still had a couple of empty blanks with just a minute to go. Desperate, I decided to copy from the answer sheet of the kid next to me. I didn't even have time to check the logic of his answers before time was called.

I felt terrible for cheating, but it was too late; the papers were passed in. Immediately I realized that I had violated the first rule of cheating: Never copy answers off of a kid who is even more clueless than you. Sadly, my seatmate's academic achievement in music class began and ended with his ability to, given three attempts, correctly distinguish a guitar from a grapefruit.

During the test review, I realized that not only were the two answers I had copied wrong, but so wrong that I and my seat partner were the only two kids in the class with those answers on our paper. Essentially, if the question had been "What are the names of two famous composers?" our answer was the equivalent of "July 4, 1776."

It didn't take the FBI to conclude that one of us had copied off of the other. Mrs. Yamada rightly determined I was the culprit and confronted me with my crime. I was humbled, contrite and humiliated. She did, however, give me a backhanded compliment: she had pegged me as the cheater because, even knowing I was dumb enough to cheat, she also knew I was not dumb enough to come up with such ridiculous answers on my own.

Seat partner sharing was encouraged in trainer rides. Evaluated as a crew, they were less quantitative than written tests. Crews were required to take a monthly trainer ride, which was recorded as pass or fail. Also, to enhance learning, frequent interaction was encouraged between the crew and instructors.

Formal trainer *evaluations* were more stressful because they were used to annually re-certify competence, to qualify for an upgraded position, or as a part of a higher headquarters inspection. Failing an evaluation meant, at the very least, a crew was temporarily de-certified to pull alert.

Evaluations were graded based not only on the number of errors a crew made, but on their magnitude. A crew could make eight minor errors and still pass. However, one critical error in EWO and the entire four-hour evaluation was a failure. Evaluations weren't letter-graded. However, an evaluator could award a crew "Outstanding Performer" status if they did especially well.

When it came to evaluations, crews were more motivated by the stick than the carrot. Being de-certified to pull alert was bad enough. To minimize impact to the alert schedule, a failed crew was immediately given additional training and then quickly thrown back in the box for a second try. If the failed evaluation was part of a command Inspector General (IG) or Nuclear Surety Inspection team visit, the crew's performance could actually cause the entire missile wing to fail the inspection. How's that for a little guilt? A missileer's saving grace was that formal evaluations were infrequent—the minimum requirement was one a year.

Every day on missile crew, in small and big ways, there was an opportunity to cheat, be it on written tests, in the trainer, or out on alert. As in every aspect of life, there are many reasons to rationalize compromising your ethics. *It won't hurt anyone. The requirement or evaluation is unfair, onerous or has little impact if not followed. Cheating will be a small risk that will avoid a potential major impact to my career, family and others.* The list goes on.

Although I never cheated on written tests or evaluations, like all missileers, on alert I didn't always do things strictly by the book. Sometimes that was for practical reasons. Other times, it was simply laziness or to avoid bad blood between myself and another crew member. I wish I had a more perfect record in that area. All it would have cost me was a little more effort and possibly some strained relationships with certain crew members—nothing I couldn't have survived.

During that first year of missile crew, my crew commander, Jake, had been going through a difficult time. If my memory serves me, it involved breaking up with his girlfriend. For whatever reason, he was very depressed. One of the things we'd been taught was to self-report emotional distress, so our mental state didn't prevent us from focusing properly on alert.

Mental focus was an important aspect of the Personnel Reliability Program (PRP). All personnel dealing directly with nuclear weapons fell under those guidelines. The program closely monitored our behavior, emotional well-being, and physical health, basically anything which could cloud our judgment. For instance, we could not take anything stronger than Tylenol without getting permission from the flight surgeon. The program was not intended to be punitive. Rather it was to protect ourselves and those we worked with from accidents.

In my crew partner's case, he was worried that his mental state would cause him to screw up on one of the monthly tests or possibly on alert. He made an appointment and shared his depression with our squadron commander. Our commander was from the old-school of leadership, intimidating and rarely confused for a soft shoulder to cry on. He thanked Jake for the honesty. Then, unbeknownst to us, he immediately directed the shop to give us a formal trainer evaluation to gauge Jake's ability to function.

Jake and I were upset when we found out. An evaluation, jokingly referred to as "an opportunity to excel," was also an opportunity to fail and face some dire consequences. This decision felt like punishment and a subtle deterrent for anyone else who might be contemplating a PRP self-report.

Decades later, I have more sympathy for our commander. Jake put him in a tough spot by revealing he had issues. If the commander didn't take action, and Jake caused an accident later, our commander could have been blamed for ignoring the warning. He also had the option of pulling Jake from alert duty temporarily. That option might have been better, but also would have been more public and caused other crew members to ask questions.

Jake's close friends, including a few evaluators, also thought the commander's decision was unfair. I resented that I was being pulled in too. I had not seen any behavior which caused me alarm about Jake's mental state. Now, added to his relationship stress was our anxiety about this unexpected evaluation.

A few days later, I drove over to the wing building for a study session. Like most missileers I didn't have a work desk or office, just a cubby hole for mail in the squadron orderly room. I checked my mail and noticed a folded piece of paper, taped at the ends. Curious, I opened it and began to read. It was a list of sequenced evaluation script events. I quickly tore the note up and threw it away. I remembered that a friend had told me earlier that he would "look out for me." I assumed he had somehow learned what was on the script and was trying to do Jake and me a favor. I was angry at his stupidity. If I had unexpectedly been caught with that paper, I could have been in hot water.

I had only read the first few lines and tried to force the content out of my head. My unknown helper might be wrong, and I didn't want my brain confused by his information while working through the evaluation. Getting the script, or "pony," ahead of time was fraught with peril. Like classroom instructors, evaluation script writers created variations of their scripts. In one, you might need to stay in the capsule and fight a fire. In another version, the indications might be changed slightly to drive a capsule evacuation. A crew had better be right, because evacuating a capsule when not required was a critical error—a failure. Yet, cheaters who had been slipped a sequence of events ahead of time would, in Air Force parlance, risk "riding the pony over the cliff." Some might be so locked in to what they thought was going to happen that they'd overlook indications presented them in the actual script and blunder into obvious errors.

Jake and I prepared the best we could in the limited time we had. Before we knew it, the evaluation was on. Thankfully, we made it through the weapons system portion and part of EWO without major errors. Then, on our last message, we hit a snag. It was unclear whether or not we had an authentic usable message directing us to launch. We were running out of allotted time to get the missiles off the ground. I thought we should turn keys, but Jake wasn't sure.

After debating while precious seconds ticked away, I glanced over at one of the evaluators. Like shop instructors, evaluators were also friends and fellow crew members. The evaluator stared at Jake and make a subtle wrist rotation. I interpreted it as a sign to turn keys. Jake turned to me and said, "I agree, let's launch." And so, we did, barely making our required time.

We passed the evaluation and neither of us ever brought up the wrist movement. Maybe I was imagining things, but I've always felt that evaluator helped us out because of Jake's situation.

Like most bad break-ups, Jake eventually got over his and we moved on. So did the parade of monthly tests, trainer rides and evaluations. Although tiring, I tried to keep it all in perspective. I was not overseas getting shot at, and every day I got to drive home, kiss my wife and play with my kids. Despite the proud tradition of missileer grousing, I was blessed.

For their part in the 2015 cheating scandal, many Malmstrom missileers received significant disciplinary action. Nine senior leaders, including the wing commander, were fired. I doubt any of them had any idea this cheating was going on.

There was much follow-on analysis as to why this scandal occurred. Several reasons were posited: low morale in the crew force because their mission was a forgotten one, the undue pressure to test at 100 percent, and the widespread crew-force opinion that test scores had little correlation to job competence. I believe there was truth in each of these explanations. In response to the scandal, the Air Force eventually announced several positive changes to crew testing. The one that caught my eye was that now, written EWO tests are to be graded only pass/fail. It will be interesting to see how long that lasts.

CHAPTER 20

North Dakota—
Vacationland USA!

All war and no play makes Cook a dull boy. When I took off the uniform, there were no more checklists to follow. No pressure to dress, act and behave like everyone else. My time was my own. Okay, it wasn't really my own. I could be called into work at any time, for any reason, the Air Force saw fit. But until the missile wing jerked the leash, I was going to run a little.

When it came to leisure time pursuits, the crew force was truly diverse. For instance, my next-door neighbor, married with no kids, spent his weekends tinkering with old cars and collecting antique toys. Another friend entered amateur rodeo competitions. Many crew members preferred escaping to the great outdoors. A running joke was that whenever commanders tried to put a positive spin on a northern tier assignment they would say, "And the hunting and fishing are great!"

True. Ice fishing was a popular North Dakota winter activity. Don't ask me why. But then again, these are the same people who get goosebumps watching the sport of curling. That competition exhibits such heart-pumping skills as gentle disc-pushing, intense staring and vigorous broom sweeping.

Unlike curling, ice fishing is more male-bonding social activity than sport. Yet, it's also the rare social activity which can lead to death. The risks begin in the pre-ice fishing commute. First, participants must either walk across, or drive their vehicle onto, a frozen lake. That's all I needed to hear before taking a pass. It gets better. Next, they cut a hole in the ice to fish through, being careful not to collapse the surrounding ice which is supporting their weight.

Finally, they erect an outhouse-like structure, called an ice hut, in which they hunker to escape the freezing wind. To enhance this party atmosphere, potent canned beverages are consumed as they huddle around a kerosene heater and wait for the fish to bite. Ice over deep water, sub-zero temperatures, kerosene and alcohol. What could possibly go wrong?

One chilly evening, after consuming multiple beers, two missileer fishing buddies accidently knocked over their heater. They watched in groggy horror as their enclosure went up in flames. They barely escaped before it burned to the ground. Arriving home with singed hair, no fish and a pile of charcoal which had once been their hut, they concluded that there were better ways to spend a weekend. Like sitting in their warm den and watching other people fish on television.

My leisure hours focused on our growing family. Beth and I arrived on base in November 1989, with one son in tow and another on the way. By early March Beth was ready to deliver. We prayed that this birth would be less stressful than Brett's six-week-early arrival. There were reasons to be confident: Beth had reached her ninth month without complications, the on-base hospital was only a few blocks away and our Air Force doctor lived just a couple of houses down from us.

Thankfully, Benjamin's birth was quick and without prolonged labor. That was also the downside. We arrived at the hospital soon after timing Beth's contractions at less than four minutes apart. During her in-processing exam, the nurses discovered she was ready to give birth—immediately.

An orderly ran to call our doctor as we helped Beth into a nearby bed. Benjamin wasn't in the waiting mood, however. There was a doctor next door in the delivery room, but he was already occupied with another birth. That left the B Team of a male nurse and Lieutenant Cook to deliver Benjamin with Beth still in her hospital bed.

Before I knew it, Beth was holding a red, wrinkled, and squalling bundle. Although the nurse expertly handled the birthing part, I performed several crucial support actions such as not fainting and randomly yelling "Push!" Despite the harried circumstances, Benjamin Kyle arrived healthy and whole. Both Beth and her nurse deserved a military medal for Outstanding Performance Under Extreme Pressure. I was happy to simply qualify for the Good Sportsmanship certificate. By the time our third child and first daughter, Victoria Ann, arrived two years later, I was a seasoned veteran of the maternity ward.

During those years, Beth and I were not alone in the family-building business. Young military couples were producing off-spring at an alarming rate. The maternity entrance to the base hospital was like a Chick-Fil-A drive-through at noon on Saturday. While providing many playmate options for my children, this also brought a serious financial burden. It seemed as though some kid was having a birthday party every ten minutes. I think half of my meager lieutenant's pay was spent on children's birthday presents and shower gifts for moms making more children for whom I would eventually need to buy gifts. Maybe China was onto something with that one child policy.

Of course, once a married couple has kids, they must find ways to entertain them. The options were limited in a state not known as Vacationland USA. We were told that Winnipeg, Canada, almost a three-hour drive north, had an impressive zoo. That turned out to be true, but the city itself seemed drab and the surrounding geography visually uninteresting, hardly worth the long drive.

I didn't want to be critical, but after living in San Diego and the beautiful Pacific Northwest, I was forever spoiled. Winnipeg's nickname was *Gateway to the West*. In my experience, most self-proclaimed gateways are code for *place you need to pass through to get where you really want to go!*

Five hours drive to the east of Grand Forks was a more attractive sightseeing option—Minneapolis. It offered professional sports and the Mall of America, a monolith which takes everything you love and hate about indoor malls and multiplies it by ten.

Minneapolis also boasted two zoos. One was the older variety that is no longer socially acceptable. It was a maze of iron bars, chain link fences and concrete. That said, you could get close enough to count a gorilla's nose hairs. Our kids loved it. The other, more modern, zoo was beautifully landscaped with animal areas that seemed to stretch for miles. Each enclosure advertised a different animal, but I could never spot one. The friendly zoo volunteers would wander over and point to some distant foliage about a quarter mile away. "See that tiger lying underneath the bush? You can make out his tail swishing and directly above, that's his left ear!" Beth and I would nod, too embarrassed to admit we could only see a bush. My theory was that the landscaping had drained the zoo budget, leaving no funds to purchase animals.

If we only had a free afternoon, Fargo was even closer—only 90 minutes away. It advertised a Roger Maris Museum in its mall. The museum turned out to be a large trophy case. Roger Maris grew up in Fargo and then became a New York Yankee baseball player. In 1961, Maris broke Babe Ruth's single-season home run record by hitting 61 round-trippers. Chasing the record was such a stressful experience, Roger's hair began to fall out. My kids weren't impressed with Roger Maris or his hair, so we moved on quickly to the Fargo Chuck E. Cheese for lunch.

Chuck E. Cheese is like Las Vegas for kids—all buzzers, flashing lights and gambling on video games. If you spent $20 on games and somehow earned 5000 tickets you could exchange them for a cheap plastic toy with a lifespan of about twenty minutes. In honor of Winnipeg, I dubbed Chuck E. Cheese, *Gateway to Dad's Wallet*. Still, the pizza was decent. Although Brett enjoyed himself, his head was on a perpetual swivel watching out for Chuck, the giant rat mascot. Brett was convinced Chuck wanted to eat him.

To reach any of these landmarks by car meant traveling long stretches of barren highway. There was little traffic, and the monotonous landscape was only punctuated by occasional clusters of homes snuggled up against a large grain elevator near railroad tracks. If you've ever seen the movie or TV series *Fargo*, you have a fairly accurate picture of the bleak environment.

I wasn't worried about kidnappers with a woodchipper (*Fargo* reference), but I didn't relish the thought of being stranded out on the highway. Especially in winter. In a bad snowstorm, a car could slide off the road into a snow drift and within minutes be invisible to passing vehicles. It was not uncommon for the news to report the discovery of people frozen to death in their cars.

Like most North Dakotans, we kept a winter emergency kit stowed in the back of our van. The kit contained blankets, flares, matches, candles (to place in a coffee can for warmth), bottled water and candy bars to eat if we were forced to survive in the vehicle for several days. I also took along several bags of kitty litter and sand, both for added weight to prevent fishtailing and to use for traction if I ever got stuck.

Fortunately, because of the brutal weather and scarce population, most North Dakota citizens are willing to stop and render assistance to any stranded motorist they encounter. Driving back to base from town one day, I hit black ice at 50 mph, spun around twice and plowed into a snowy ditch. I was unhurt but shaken. Almost immediately, two community members pulled over and used chains and their pickups to tow me out.

When we weren't on hazardous roads, back at the base we still enjoyed the same seasonal activities as any young family in America. Yet, experiencing them up north added a new dimension. In Virginia, kids don't normally trudge through snow on Halloween. Our junior superheroes and princesses were so layered with gloves, hats, coats and scarves that their trick or treat identities had to be taken on faith. For New Englanders this is nothing new, but it was uncharted territory for this Navy brat.

At Christmas, Santa Claus arrived by military helicopter outside the golf course clubhouse and distributed treats to the base kids. Santa was surprisingly buff for an old man and kept using non-elf phrases like "Let me stow my gear first" and "You kids line up in formation." I surmised that Santa could hop a helicopter because the North Pole was so close to the base.

Enduring the long winters required creativity. One Valentine's Day the weather was too foul for Beth and me to venture into town for a romantic dinner. So, after the kids were in bed, I snuck down to the basement and filled their large plastic swimming pool with steaming hot water and bubble bath. Then, I surrounded it with plastic plants, hung Christmas lights overhead, turned out the lights and put on Hawaiian music. Beth and I donned our swimsuits, slipped into the water and pretended we were on a tropical island honeymoon. It was quite romantic until one of the locals pushed through the plants and announced that his brother had peed the bed. Where is the resort housekeeping staff when you need them?

When April arrived, the pre-spring anticipation on base was more like the run-up to Christmas. As temps pushed up into the low 50s, everyone declared winter over. Neighbors gathered in sandals and Hawaiian shirts, threw open their garage doors and fired up the barbeque grills.

When sun and green colors finally arrived, our misery wasn't over. Melting snow raised the local Red River to dangerous levels. The river divided downtown Grand Forks, North Dakota, from East Grand Forks, Minnesota. During my crew time, the base populace's first rite of spring was helping the community stack thousands of sandbags to block the rising river. Most years this effort was successful. In 1997, it was not enough. That spring, the banks overflowed and downtown Grand Forks became a lake with dozens of homes and businesses destroyed. Even the local high school flooded, compelling the Air Force to rescue their senior prom by inviting them to hold it in a base aircraft hangar.

Like the biblical plagues of Egypt, after the flooding came the standing water and mosquitoes. I'd lived in the southern United States but had never seen mosquitoes like North Dakota mosquitoes. There's a reason why the mosquito is the unofficial state bird. They were everywhere. Outfielders at base softball games used their ball gloves to shield their faces from attack, peering at the action between the leather fingers. At home, mowing the lawn required a long sleeve shirt and jeans with *Off!* sprayed on any uncovered skin area. After being cooped up all winter, it didn't seem fair that we couldn't enjoy the outdoors, even in summer.

Despite the challenging climate, the people I worked with were wonderful. I've never had closer friends or greater camaraderie than at Grand Forks. One summer when our family was camping in Ohio, basements flooded across base housing. My coworkers, despite dealing with their own watery mess, checked out our key from the housing office and without our even knowing it, cleaned up our basement and dragged every soggy item upstairs to the garage to dry out. You never forget friends like that.

Those in the local community were also solid people. They were family-oriented, resilient, non-complaining, hard-working folks. Although somewhat stand-offish socially, they were quick to help a stranger in need. We all benefited from raising families in a place where crime was rare. During the winter, restaurant patrons would leave their vehicles unlocked and running in the parking lot so the engine block wouldn't freeze up. No one worried about theft. The last year I was on crew a little girl was abducted in Fargo. Although tragic, that kind of crime was almost unheard of in the area.

Base leadership also did their part to make the assignment more enjoyable. Each squadron sponsored a variety of social activities such as picnics, bowling nights and even cross-town scavenger hunts. During one particularly memorable hunt, we were tasked to dive to the bottom of the Grand Forks YMCA pool to retrieve an item. Although some of these activities fell under the dreaded category of "mandatory fun," many were a blast. One event Beth and I particularly enjoyed was the Dining-Out.

An Air Force Dining-Out is a formal dinner (or mess) for military members and their guests. It involves solemn military toasts and remembrances as well as humorous punishments for violating a long list of semi-serious mess rules. Any military member caught breaking a rule is called out to the entire assembly and sent to the grog bowl to perform penance by performing a toast. If that toast is not executed precisely in word and deed, then the wrongdoer is punished again.

This is immensely entertaining as long as you aren't the violator. The grog bowl is typically either a punch bowl or even an actual toilet bowl (unused) filled with a disgusting concoction of ingredients mixed with alcohol. For more sedate affairs, there is also an "unleaded" (non-alcoholic) grog bowl with a more benign punch mixture.

Once sent to the grog bowl, the accused is required to fill his or her glass, toast the mess, then down the contents of the glass, including ice cubes, in one continuous gulp. Next, to demonstrate the contents are gone, the glass must be placed upside down over the head. Finally, the offender must perform a proper facing movement before marching back to their seat. Rank has no privilege in the mess with brave second lieutenants frequently calling violations on their commanders. However, if the accuser flubs the accusation speech, he or she will then be ordered to join the accused at the grog bowl.

Overseeing all this activity is the President of the Mess, typically the senior officer in attendance. The President does little beyond hosting the head table and making final judgments. The real work is performed by the Vice, who sits at the back of the room, facing the head table. This junior officer is kept hopping, doing the President's bidding, narrating the script and keeping order in what can be a raucous environment.

There are boundaries. Everything must be done in fun and good taste. Following are a few of the typical mess rules.

1. Thou shalt not be late to the mess. (I was once sent to the grog bowl for this violation. In my defense, my tardiness was caused by my guest, to whom I happened to be married.)

2. Thou shalt not leave the mess whilst convened. Military protocol overrides all calls of nature.

3. Thou shalt not murder the Queen's English.

4. Thou shalt not open the hangar doors (talk shop).

5. Thou shalt fall into disrepute with thy peers if the pleats of thy cummerbund are inverted (reminder: pleats should be facing up so you can catch falling crumbs).

6. Thou shalt also be painfully regarded if thy clip-on bow tie rides at an obvious list (harder to avoid than it sounds).

7. Thou shalt not laugh at ridiculously funny comments unless the President first shows approval by laughing.

8. Thou shalt not question the decisions of the President.

9. Thou shalt consume thy meal in a manner becoming gentle-persons.

10. Thou shalt express thy approval by tapping thy spoon on the table. Clapping of thy hands will not be tolerated.

11. Thou shalt not write long chapters which test thy readers' patience. (I just added that one.)

CHAPTER 21

The Missile Olympics

Bless their hearts. In the mid–1960s, Strategic Air Command (SAC) leadership became increasingly concerned about low morale in the missile crew force. During the psychedelic era of flowing hair, peace and love, it wasn't cool to be a tapered in the back, hair off the ears, uniform wearing, Air Force launch officer. The *happening scene* was on the mellow sun-kissed coast of California or in the high-energy cities, not the windy wheat fields of the upper Midwest. Because of the Vietnam War, it wasn't cool to be in the military—period. Worse yet, in the Air Force itself, it wasn't even cool to be a missileer. Pilots were the virtual big men on the military campus. So, how to buck up the crew force?

I can imagine that one snowy Nebraska evening a general at SAC Headquarters had an epiphany. Why not create an annual missile competition similar to the one for bomber pilots? That event generated fierce rivalry as air crews battled it out for recognition as the best at putting bombs on target. *Heck*, thought the general, *we'll even hold this missile competition at Vandenberg AFB and award trophies. Give those poor toads a couple weeks to thaw out in the California sun.*

So, in 1967, SAC's Missile Combat Competition, nicknamed "Olympic Arena," was born. The objectives were as follows: (1) refine current procedures and techniques, (2) promote the exchange of professional information among personnel from SAC missile units, (3) increase recognition of outstanding SAC individuals, wings and non–SAC participating agencies and (4) enhance esprit de corps throughout the SAC ICBM force. Well, three out of four ain't bad.

Full disclosure—I was never an Olympic Arena participant. But I knew several coworkers who were. From what I recall, their personal objectives were slightly different from SAC's. They wanted to (1) gain recognition to enhance promotion opportunities, (2) escape Grand Forks for two weeks and (3) gain recognition to enhance promotion opportunities. I had no problem with those goals. More power to them. However, to me, and many of the crew force, the additional study and practice time wasn't worth

126

the potential reward. Let's just say there was not a bull rush to sign up for try-outs.

The actual competition would be performed in the trainer, not on a real site—another reason for the lack of Olympic Arena fever. There would be no fans cheering in the stands, no Soviet counterparts hurling insults from across dueling consoles. Not even the thrill of launching a real missile. That experience was offered only on annual Glory Trips.

A Glory Trip was referred to formally as a Follow-On Test and Evaluation (FOTE) and culminated in the live launch of an on-alert missile. Each year, a Minuteman III was randomly selected from the missile fields up north. First, the weaponed reentry vehicle was removed. The missile was then pulled from its launch tube and trucked to Vandenberg Air Force Base. Here it was placed in a silo and fitted with test equipment and dummy warheads. Two lucky crews from the missile's squadron were selected to travel out to California, set-up operations in the test underground launch control center and launch the missile downrange.

The test launch environment differed from that of a real-world North Dakota launch. Instead of two launch crews operating from separate capsules, all four crew members worked together in the same location and took turns providing the required four launch votes. Also, since this was only a test, a mission flight control officer (MFCO) sat on console at another base location ready to blow up the missile if it began to fly off course.

Once launched, the test Minuteman III traveled over 4,700 miles across the Pacific Ocean, a distance roughly equivalent to reaching Russia from North Dakota. At the business end of the launch, three dummy warheads would come screaming out of the sky aimed at a pre-determined target area off the coast of the Kwajalein Atoll, over 2000 miles southwest of Hawaii. The ballistic arc resembled a long high lob with the missile reportedly reaching an apogee of 750 miles in space. That's over three times higher than the International Space Station's orbit around the earth.

The test was intended to validate that our on-alert missiles both worked and were accurate. It was also a literal shot across the bow to our Soviet friends, who we assumed were watching from nearby "fishing" trawlers. The message? The United States is ready and able to meet any aggression—don't test us!

What the test launch didn't measure was the crew's ability to react to an unplanned and unexpected launch order. At Vandenberg, the missileers knew well ahead of time when they were required to turn keys. Still, the four officers were joining a select club of missileers who had gained real-world launch experience.

I would have loved to go on a Glory Trip, but the timing never worked

Minuteman III missile, minus warhead, test-launched over the Pacific Ocean from Vandenberg Air Force Base (U.S. Air Force).

out. When our squadron's turn came around, I was in the shop and not eligible for selection.

Olympic Arena's simulated launches couldn't compare to the visceral thrill of a Glory Trip. Yet, if *career* glory was your aim, experience as a missile combat competitor was the way to go. With an annual performance report line that read "Led the 321st Strategic Missile Wing Olympic Arena team in winning the Blanchard Trophy," it wouldn't matter if the rest of the sheet was left blank. No other crew member was going to top that accolade.

For the rest of us non-competitors at the wing, our morale was to be boosted by the excitement of tracking our fellow crew members' performance and the pride of, hopefully, seeing them lift the Blanchard Trophy.

Yet, during Olympic Arena season, the apathy was almost palpable. We certainly wished our competing friends well in California but felt little vicarious connection to their fate. Few of us huddled around the closed-circuit television broadcasts with fingers crossed, breathlessly riveted on the score posting. We did not view the other missile wings as archrivals to be vanquished. Grand Forks wasn't the University of Michigan, Minot wasn't the University of Southern California, and Olympic Arena was not the Rose Bowl. Missileers at the other five missile wings were just fellow slobs like us, trying to carve out a decent Air Force career. Missileers complained; we didn't talk trash.

I did admire those who put themselves out there to compete. There was ample opportunity for humiliation as well as glory. The Olympic Arena missile trainer scripts were difficult and designed to trip up even the best. There were simulated mishaps, fires, medical emergencies, equipment malfunctions and problems piled on top of problems to overwhelm, distract and confuse. And that was just in the opening five minutes.

These evil scenarios were devised by evaluators deep within the bowels of the 3901st Strategic Missile Evaluations Squadron (SMES). Their officers were former missileers who now worked at Vandenberg and were tasked with traveling to the missile wings each year and administering brutal evaluations on behalf of SAC Headquarters. They were selected for this shameful duty based on three criteria: (1) superior weapon system knowledge, (2) owning the blackest of hearts and (3) having no discernible souls.

To take on the SMES, pronounced "smeez" (or, behind their backs, "sleeze"), a competitor needed to hit the books. Each wing had a cadre of Olympic Arena trainers who put their teams through their paces in the weeks leading up to competition. One of the competitors' reference documents was the Olympic Arena Study Manual, 65 pages of warnings, tips and techniques to be memorized. Here is an excerpt from the 1992 version:

> You have an MF fire; first isolation action is to trip the transmit circuit breaker (CB). As soon as you trip that CB, the receiver CB trips. This NOT a self-isolating fire. Take a time hack on the receiver CB; ask the (evaluator) status of the fire one minute from tripping the transmit CB. If the smoke dissipates you know it is not self-isolating for the smoke wouldn't have dissipated until one minute from the receiver tripping. Reset the receiver after monitoring for 2 minutes.

You can see why it might be difficult to keep 65 pages of this stuff from leaking out of your ears.

To be fair, the SMES had their own challenges creating trainer scripts that were equitable among the six missile wings. Not all the wings had the same missiles (Peacekeeper vs Minuteman) or even the same versions of the same missile (Minuteman II and Minuteman III). Whiteman Air Force Base was the only base that had the Emergency Rocket Communication System (ERCS) on a select number of their missiles. These would be launched, not with weapons, but with recorded radio messages as a survivable means to direct the missile wings in wartime.

We at Grand Forks and our sister "Deuce" squadron at Malmstrom Air Force Base had the most complicated operating system. Our Minuteman III was capable of carrying up to three independently targeted warheads, which made retargeting dicier. The Minuteman II version at other bases could only carry one warhead. We were able to retarget all of our missiles from the capsule. Another system still required a maintenance team to travel out to each missile site and load new targeting there.

The major complexity of Grand Fork's system was that instead of a redundant underground cable system for computers to communicate between the capsule and missiles, we had a single cable line and a radio system. That meant we had to track and account for issues with two different systems. Radio communication was especially spotty in the summer months because of thunderstorms.

This situation gave SMES evaluators an opportunity to trip up Grand Forks and Malmstrom Deuce system competitors by inserting scenarios involving multiple cable breaks coupled with radio outages causing certain missiles' status to be unknown. In those instances, crews were required to quickly turn over missile responsibility to another capsule which because of geographic location could still "see" the missile. If not, a maintenance crew had to be dispatched to the missile silo to safe the missile—keep it from accepting any launch commands.

By the time our competitors were ready to leave for California, we were cautioned to not administer any congratulatory back slaps in case their heads, stuffed with information, exploded from the impact.

At most bases, the final pre-competition event was a mandatory wing-wide pep rally for the team. The energy was pumped up with blaring rock music (think Bad Company and Van Halen) and hearty unit cheers led by supervisors taking note of those who failed to display the proper level of coerced spontaneous enthusiasm. Up on stage, the competitors fidgeted awkwardly, all lined up in their matching ball caps and jackets. The fervor seemed more than a little forced and most of the competitors, although worthy of admiration, were ill at ease playing the role of star athlete.

Everyone was glad when the send-off was over, including the competitors. The military does formal ceremony well. Pep rallies, however, are not a core competency. The military shines in the solemn pageantry of parades, funerals and events such as medal award ceremonies, change of commands or flag folding demonstrations. I am often moved when attending these. Even retirement ceremonies frequently elicit tears from the most grizzled of troops as they face taking off the uniform for the last time. While the world has gone Casual Friday on us, the military, and some churches, seem to be the last bastion of public formality and reverence.

There was certainly formality in the Olympic Arena score posting—a nightly Vandenberg event where all competitors gathered in a large auditorium to cheer and cajole as smartly-dressed non-commissioned officers (NCOs) revealed the day's results. Per tradition, the NCOs performed their duties with a stone-faced glare that was either reminiscent of a murder conviction announcement or the intense suppression of gastric emissions. They marched expertly across the stage and with solemn dignity, ascended platforms and hung numbers on a giant scoreboard. To add a dash of theatrics, all scores were posted slowly, one digit at a time. Some NCOs would pause after each digit and glare out into the audience until the crowd, in a fever pitch, cajoled him into continuing.

In addition to the score posting and actual competition, the week also boasted a bevy of group cheers, cook-outs, photo opportunities, senior officer motivational speeches and improvised entertainment by each wing's mascot. Yes, there were mascots. A group mascot photo from the 1980s shows, among others, a Viking, frontiersman, cowboy and two fuzzy creatures of unknown origin.

All this excitement was too much to not share with other career fields in SAC. Within a few years of the first Olympic Arena, competition was added for security forces and missile maintainers. Later, even vehicle maintenance crews and cooks were added. I'm all for being inclusive, but I thought the additions went too far. I'm not convinced that determining the best burrito-maker in SAC is good use of taxpayer dollars.

In 1993, after the ICBM force joined with space operations under Air Force Space Command, space operators were added to the competition, and it was re-named Guardian Challenge. Again, I had questions. For instance, what about the space launch competition between Patrick AFB and Vandenberg AFB officers? That seemed curious since, although Air Force officers sat on console for launches, Boeing and Lockheed Martin contractors monitored and controlled the rocket's functions. What did that leave the space launch crews to compete in—quickest to evacuate the area during a rocket explosion? Yet, it was negative attitudes like mine that this competition was created to combat.

Sadly, during my four years on crew, Grand Forks never won the Blanchard Trophy. Yet, I don't recall that loss impacting my morale. The frequent explanation was that because we had the most complicated missile system, we were at a competitive disadvantage. That was our story anyway. Maybe if we had won the Blanchard, I would have experienced a surge in career pride. Maybe I would have strutted past B1-B bomber pilots in the BX parking lot and with shoulders back and jaw firmly set, said "Yes, I'm a missileer, and I'm darn proud of it." We'll never know.

Yet, even public pride in our missile competition had its limits. One year the instructor office came up with a monthly crew force self-study cover which advertised the upcoming missile competition. The cover had the Olympic Arena emblem and simply stated underneath, "No pilots required," a true and fairly benign statement. The self-study was distributed to the crew force and no one gave it a second thought. Until our 321st Operations Group commander, the third most senior wing officer, called the instructor shop chief into his office. The colonel felt that the cover disparaged air crews and said we needed to get rid of them—the covers, not the air crews. He wasn't joking and it wasn't April Fool's Day.

So, the shop chief directed all 200 missileers to tear off the offensive covers from their self-study and turn them into his office. Later, I found one and kept it as a souvenir. I doubt any pilots on base were aware of these covers or would have cared if they were. Life is strange, but sometimes life in the Air Force is even stranger.

CHAPTER 22

The Pit vs. the Cockpit

To state the obvious, the focus of the Air Force is flying airplanes. It's right there in the motto, "Fly, Fight and Win." It doesn't state, "Fly, Fight, Launch Missiles, Maintain Personnel Records and Win." Although missiles, space assets and even unmanned aerial systems (UAS) are also key mission–contributors, the Air Force world still revolves around piloted-aircraft.

Almost every job on an Air Force base from security to finance to maintenance originated out of the need to support aircraft, airfields and pilots. Even when the Air Force operated satellites, most orbited the earth to ensure pilots and air operations centers could communicate and maintain situational awareness of targets and threats. Intercontinental ballistic missiles like the Minuteman III? They were employed as an option to strike targets that ether could not be quickly reached by aircraft or were located at points too risky for a plane. These facts are well-understood by the Air Force community. Not everyone gets to be Batman. Some must be Robins, Commissioner Gordons, or even Alfred the Butlers.

Some non-pilots resent this reality. Many of them had dreamed of being Maverick from the *Top Gun* movie, clad in aviator sunglasses and leather jacket, speeding down the flight line on a motorcycle with beautiful Kelly McGinnis clutching their torso from behind.

It never bothered me that I wasn't a pilot. After teaching P.E. at boarding school, serving as an Air Force officer, even a missileer, was a big step up in excitement. The wild blue yonder held no allure for me personally. I'm not sure why. Everyone assumed that I chose the Air Force because I wanted to fly. It's not that I couldn't envision the adrenaline rush of tearing through the sky in an F-16. But piloting most aircraft in the Air Force inventory was analogous to driving a bus. Typical pilots transport people and stuff from point A to point B. In between, they sit for hours in the cockpit, staring out at the clouds or rechecking their instruments. Granted, unlike a bus driver, if there's engine trouble, a pilot can't just pull over to the curb and walk away. Still, the thought of flying didn't get my blood pumping.

I was in the minority. It appeared that a not insignificant segment of the missile crew force had at one time hoped to become pilots. Some committed to the Air Force, but ultimately weren't selected for pilot training. These officers often felt compelled to explain why they weren't flying aircraft. Even if no one asked. God was usually the culprit. He had cursed them with bad eyesight or some other physical limitation, which, through no fault of their own, derailed what certainly would have been a soaring career. No doubt. Yet, I resented the perception by some that there were only two types of officers: pilots and those who wished they were.

Other would-be pilots were initially selected but washed out of training before earning their wings. A crushing blow, I'm sure. Yet, the cruelest fate was reserved for the so called "banked pilots." This unhappy group had successfully completed the arduous flight training only to learn upon graduation that there weren't any flying assignments available. The Air Force had over-recruited in certain years and was left with more pilots than cockpits.

So, they "banked" these officers for a rainy day by shuttling them off to other assignments until a flying job opened up. Some ended up as missileers in an underground North Dakota launch control center. Sadly, Kelly McGinnis was not hugging them down there. Banked pilot morale was about as low as their buried capsules.

For officers without a seat at the cool table in the Air Force cafeteria, it's easy to be jealous. For starters, pilots make more money than their non-flying counterparts. Pilots receive additional monthly flight pay, hazardous duty pay when they deploy, and in many cases, are offered substantial bonuses to re-up in the military. When missileers choose to leave the service, they are typically thanked, offered a hearty handshake and shown the door.

Pilots also have a reputation for feeling entitled and acting arrogant. To be fair, that has not been my experience with them. I've certainly run across a few who were lacking in humility, but not necessarily any more than I've encountered within my own career field. Most pilots I've known are more Sully than Maverick.

My best friend at Squadron Officer's School was a southern gentleman who happened to be an F-16 pilot. Two of the nicest and most humble officers I ever met were KC-135 tanker pilots. Don't misunderstand, though. Pilots are confident individuals. They have to be to do what they do. When I'm on a flight, I don't want the crew in the cockpit to be second-guessing themselves each time they move the yoke. I'll excuse supreme confidence, even a little arrogance, in my pilot, brain surgeon and Navy Seal rescuer.

The pilots I knew had little patience for the bureaucracy and administrivia of the Air Force. Their focus was on the immediate, the hands-on, the practical. This can create irritation in their Air Force comrades who labor in more administrative-driven areas, where staffing procedures are law and five written approvals are required before blowing your nose.

I saw first-hand how pilots approached staff work during my assignment at the Air Force Doctrine Center. With fliers in charge, formal staff packages containing a half dozen tabs and multiple levels of approval went out the window. Major revisions to service doctrine publications, eventually signed off by the Chief of Staff of the Air Force, were primarily coordinated by junior officers via e-mail. I couldn't believe it. Yet, in the minds of my senior leadership, it wasn't a big deal. Unlike a plane crash, no lives would be lost because a few colonels had failed to sign off on a doctrine revision. Maybe they had a point.

Even little things peculiar to pilot culture could be off-putting for those who served outside the velvet rope. Call signs for instance. Early in their careers, it is customary for pilots to be christened with a nickname or "call sign." These aren't just used among friends. Most pilots encourage everyone they encounter to address them by their call sign. They even have them printed on their flight suit name tags and use them in their correspondence signature blocks. To me, it felt odd to address one set of officers as Major Jones or Captain Smith, but refer to pilots as "Crash," "Beans" or "Nails."

Some call signs are humorous, especially if they are a pun on the pilot's last name. For instance, a Major General Looney went by the call sign "Tunes." Other call signs were awarded for some obscure training or dive bar incident that the average person would not understand unless given the backstory. Often it was better not to ask.

The missile crew force didn't have a call sign tradition. The nicknames we called each were usually not ones the owner would use in an e-mail signature.

During Vandenberg missile training, we learned that one of our instructors had a call sign of sorts. His fellow instructors had christened him, "Banister Bill." Curious, we inquired as to the origin of that name. The other instructors refused to say. Instead, they cautioned us to never ever, under any circumstances, call him "Banister" or to ask him how he received his nickname. Since we all wanted to graduate, we never did. Speculation was that, spurred on by excess alcohol, our instructor had decided to slide down a hotel banister. Reaching the bottom at high speed, he slammed into the end post, permanently injuring a very crucial and sensitive part of his anatomy.

Despite the call sign divide and others, pilots and missileers at Grand Forks shared some experiences. Both groups were stuck in the same, less-than-desirable base assignment. You might be a cool pilot, but you were still a cool pilot living in Grand Forks, North Dakota. Fliers had to shovel their cars out of snow drifts, just like we did. For excitement, all of us drove the wife and kids to the mall for shopping and dinner at the Grand Fork Buffet.

Both groups had an internal pecking order. On the flying side, fighter pilots were clearly at the top, followed by pilots of certain reconnaissance aircraft and bombers. Below them were everyone else, including the transport and tanker pilots. I'm not sure where helicopter pilots fell. They seemed to be in their own distinct category.

Grand Forks had a flight of UH-1 "Huey" helicopters. Earlier versions of these aircraft were employed during the Vietnam War for a variety of combat missions including air assault and aeromedical evacuation. By my time on crew, "N" versions were flying at all the missile bases. In their missile base mission, these versatile aircraft transported security and emergency response personnel, performed search and rescue missions and supported off-base nuclear weapon convoys.

One of their secondary tasks was transporting missile crews out to alert sites when roads were impassable in bad weather. To get flight hours, the helicopter pilots would fly a few crews out to their sites each month. Typically, they transported two crews at a time, dropping each one off at their assigned launch control facility. On one such trip, my crew partner and I were dropped off last. As we approached our site, my partner made the mistake of asking the pilot if he ever practiced any "cool maneuvers."

"Hold tight," he responded. Then, still high and almost directly above our landing site, he thrust the bird into a fast, deep, circling dive. I felt like I was in a tornado of swirling water heading towards a toilet drain. It was quite exhilarating compared to our normal approach, rolling up in a 1986 Chevy Suburban. Exciting that is, until I felt my breakfast shoving its way towards my throat. I believe that was the pilot's intention. When finally safe on terra firma, my partner and I wobbled unsteadily off toward the support building. The pilot grinned and waved good-bye. I wondered what fun he had in mind for the off-going crew who would be flying back with him.

The one responsibility shared between Grand Forks missileers and the bomber and tanker pilots was pulling strategic alert. Like us, these fliers were required to be ready at a moment's notice to respond to a nuclear attack.

The B-1B bomber was first deployed at Grand Forks in the mid–1980s. The Air Force intended for the new bomber to be an upgrade and possible eventual replacement for the B-52. They were half right. Over 35 years later, the B-52 is still going strong, flying crucial missions throughout the Air Force. The B1-B was reported to be much faster, more maneuverable and far more capable of penetrating enemy radar. If ordered by the president, the B1-B was capable of taking off within minutes, loaded with weapons and heading towards either an assigned holding pattern or overseas target. Supporting the bomber's air to air refueling needs was the KC-135 tanker, also stationed at Grand Forks and assigned strategic alert.

As with missileers, alert flight crews were tasked with receiving, decoding and authenticating Emergency War Order messages to determine their actions. Unsurprisingly, a flight crew's alert was very different from a missile launch crew's. A flight crew pulled alert seven straight days, one week out of every month. Our schedule was typically eight alerts a month, each 24 hours long.

While our alert sites were anywhere from a 40 minute to 2.5-hour drive from base, the flight crew alert facility was on base, adjacent to the flight line. The alert facility was a long rectangular concrete apron, surrounded by a fence, near the end of the airfield. It was guarded around the clock by armed security forces. The alert aircraft were parked inside the fence, fueled and ready to fly. Nearby were concrete bunkers where the alert crews lived during their week of duty.

Although flight crews pulled longer alerts than missileers, they had more freedom. They could easily socialize with not only their own crew, but others inside the fence. They were allowed outside for fresh air and were even afforded outdoor recreational opportunities. Some bases built basketball courts and swimming pools within their alert facilities.

If a flight crew became bored inside the fence, they were allowed to take an alert vehicle (government van) and drive to pre-approved destinations on base. It was not unusual to see alert crews at the library, gymnasium, personnel office, arts and crafts center, etc.

One of the big attractions to these outings was the ability to meet with spouses, kids and significant others. These get-togethers were still within sight and earshot of the other crew members, but it was better than an entire week of separation.

Of course, such field trips could be interrupted at any moment by a base-wide klaxon signaling the crews to scramble to their aircraft. To facilitate a quick return to the flight line, most base facilities had reserved parking spaces near the entrance for alert vehicles. Moreover, along base streets leading to the airfield, there were also flashing lights which compelled all other traffic to pull over and allow speeding alert vehicles to pass.

Once inside the alert facility, crews would literally run to their aircraft, a scene reproduced in many Hollywood war movies. For the on-base populace, watching speeding alert vehicles and the subsequent conga line of aircraft taking off would be quite the show. Except for what it all meant. And what it meant was an impending attack from enemy missiles, probably streaking towards targets like Grand Forks Air Force Base.

For families and base personnel, there was little hope of seeking refuge. I don't recall if the base even had a bomb shelter. I also don't recall ever having a conversation with Beth about what she would do if I was on alert and a nuclear war kicked off. Maybe it was our optimistic belief that such a thing would never happen. Or maybe we both knew that nothing could be done anyway, so why discuss it. I assume she would have gathered our three children, huddled in the basement and prayed. Luckily, we never had to find out.

Later in my career, the Air Force eliminated the distinctive blue flight suit worn exclusively by missileers and space operators. To engender a greater feeling of one Air Force operations team, all operators, not just flight crews, were issued the green flight suit. Now, unless you were up close and saw the distinctive missile badge on the name patch, missileers looked just like pilots. The Air Force even issued us the coveted leather bomber jacket, which we could keep. I'm not sure how pilots felt about all this, but I can imagine. The green flight suit was fine, but I kind of missed the old blue bag. It was an easy way to spot a fellow missileer on base or at conferences. I was more enthused about the bomber jacket. Still wear mine today. Eat your heart out, Maverick!

CHAPTER 23

The Monster in the Drawer

I was not overly stressed during my four years of missile crew. Like most of my peers, I considered nuclear war a remote possibility. Also, it was virtually impossible for a missile operations crew to accidentally launch or disable a missile. So, those scenarios weren't great concerns.

What did concern me was possibly making a career-impacting mistake. An officer can't spend four years on missile crew without messing up. Everyone's human. All one can hope for is that the inevitable mistake doesn't harm anyone, degrade national security or hurt their own career.

There were four basic areas where a missileer could really "step in it," as airmen often say. The first was mishandling classified information; the second, accidently taking a missile off alert; third, allowing a security breach and fourth; risking personnel safety. On every 24-hour alert there was ample opportunity to do one or all four.

Because of my Top Secret security clearance, I was frequently tasked with briefing, handling, transporting, checking, protecting or reviewing classified information—information which, if compromised, could do grave damage to the nation. Because missile procedures involved both classified and unclassified information, it was easy to momentarily forget where those distinctions were. A missileer was always one slip of the tongue away from trouble.

Trouble lurked in other areas as well. Classified information sometimes had to be couriered from one secure location to another. As a crew, we frequently carried classified with us from the base to our alert location. If you misplaced the documents, allowed an uncleared person to see them, or didn't employ the proper controls (some handling required two people with "eyes on" at all times) you were in deep trouble. In a subsequent assignment, a co-worker and I were tasked with transporting classified documents in a briefcase on a six-hour car trip from Alabama to Florida. I was never happier in my life than when we finally locked those documents in the Florida base's safe.

Even in the secure launch control center, you were not off the hook.

Before a new crew took over an alert, they were required to inventory all the classified material in the capsule filing cabinet. If anything was missing, a security compromise had to be immediately reported. Then, the investigators would determine if the material had been misplaced, lost, or even worse, stolen.

Of course, for a missileer with traitorous intentions, removing classified documents was not necessary. It was simple enough to copy down classified information in a notebook or take photos of documents while a crew partner slept. That's why the Air Force required that we pass background investigations. Their best protection against a security compromise was a crew force of trustworthy individuals.

No crew member was ever charged with spying during my tour at Grand Forks. However, I endured ribbing during my initial Emergency War Order training at Vandenberg, because of a missileer who was charged. As reported in the *New York Times*, in 1981, Second Lieutenant Christopher Cooke turned over classified Titan II ICBM material to officials at the Soviet Embassy in New York. The information was detailed and damaging. So damaging that, according to the article, the Air Force was forced to immediately change missile targets and codes on several Titan II missiles.

When Lieutenant Cooke was ultimately caught, he claimed his motive in passing the information was to gain the Soviets' trust, so he could then pull even more valuable information out of them. So, I guess his heart was in the right place.

As a final twist of the knife, in the run-up to his court-martial, the Air Force made mistakes in offering Cooke partial immunity in return for his inventory of exactly what he had turned over. In the United States Military Court of Appeals review, his case was overturned and his guilty conviction thrown out. Lieutenant Cooke walked away a free man to pursue other life goals. I can imagine that if he had been a Russian missileer in the same situation, he very likely would have been dragged to an underground bunker and never heard from again. Although I kept pointing out that my last name did not end in "e," I was continually asked how my traitor cousin was doing.

Even the most patriotic missileers were susceptible to inadvertently mishandling classified material. One Grand Forks crew received unwanted attention when they failed to properly destroy a code stream. In those days, after alert, the departing crew carried their expired code streams with them topside into the security control center. After the flight security controller was directed to the back of the room, the crew would destroy these paper code streams. To accomplish this, they used two authorized pieces of sophisticated equipment—a cigarette lighter and a coffee can. Once the code stream was burned in the can, the charred remains were further mashed up to ensure no recognizable code letters remained.

This was all fairly routine—and that was the danger. On one occasion as my friends burned their codes, someone unexpectedly entered the room, allowing a gust of wind to sweep through. Momentarily distracted, they failed to notice a small single piece of charred code stream float up out of the burn can and fall onto the floor. Thinking they had all the pieces, the crew returned to their task and mashed the remaining ashes. They then bid the flight security controller farewell and drove back to base, anticipating a relaxing afternoon at home.

Unknown to them, soon after they departed, the security controller (uncleared for those codes) discovered the lone piece of half-burned code stream with a couple visible letters. He immediately called in a security situation and reports went flying. Upon dropping off their equipment back at base, the surprised crew was pulled into their commander's office. There they endured a verbal torching that would have put their cigarette lighter to shame. I heard they were given letters of counseling which were filed in their official records, directed to complete many hours of remedial code-handling training and finally ordered to brief the entire squadron on what led to their error and the steps they were taking to ensure it would never happen again.

This was overkill, in my mind. These were good guys who made an honest mistake. They didn't need retraining on procedures. What was left of the code stream was certainly useless and never even left a secure area. However, it didn't matter. It was a security breach in procedure and a message needed to be sent to the crew force: *Don't screw up. Next time, this could be you.*

Although not formal punishment, additional training was almost always assigned to crews who messed up. Sometimes the entire crew force was assigned the same remedial training, which made the offending crew feel even worse.

Formal punishment ran the gamut. For serious offenses like sexual abuse, misuse of funds, theft, etc., an officer was criminally charged and tried before a military judge or panel (jury) in a court-martial. If found guilty, offenders could be sentenced to years of prison in the United States Disciplinary Barracks at Fort Leavenworth in Kansas.

For less severe offenses, commanders could administer nonjudicial punishment, such as an Article 15 where the offender might be suspended without pay for a period of time, assigned additional work, or restricted to base.

More typical for the crew force were lower levels of punishment. Everyone loves getting mail, but no officer wanted the types of letters that could end up in an official file. The least severe of these letters was a letter of counseling. The most serious was a letter of reprimand. Some merciful commanders, instead of filing the letters in the offender's permanent record simply put them "in the drawer." Then, the offender was given a probationary period. At the end of the stated period, if the person had not repeated the offense, the commander would remove the letter and destroy it.

I made it through almost four years and 240 alerts before I became a "man of letters," for the first and only time. On alert one afternoon, I somehow missed an outer zone security light popping on for one of my missile sites. Therefore, I failed to dispatch the topside armed response team to respond. In my defense, there were maintenance issues in the capsule which allowed several adjacent panel lights to constantly cycle on and off. In the midst of that distracting light show, this one security light came on for several minutes and then reset. I never noticed it.

On a normal day, no one outside the capsule would have known that I'd missed the light. It was common for outer zone lights to be triggered during an alert. With rare exceptions it was caused by a non-hostile event such as a computer malfunction, wind, rolling tumbleweeds or small animals crawling through the fence.

Unfortunately for me, the light I missed was caused by a human being, although a friendly one. A security forces officer was driving around the missile field and wanted to observe our security team's response to unknown movement within the launch facility fence line. Without pre-coordinating with me, he unlocked the gate to one of my missile sites, walked in and triggered the movement sensor. Sometimes security officers didn't pre-coordinate these exercises because they feared the capsule crew would tip off their topside armed response teams that a supervisor was testing their reaction. Anyway, assuming I would see the corresponding light and call the security situation, the security captain backed off site in his truck and waited for the response team to arrive. And waited and waited.

When he realized no one was coming, he called down to the capsule and asked if I had called a security situation 6A at LF-XX. I said no, then checked my printout record and, to my chagrin, saw a "301" indicating the outer zone light had gone off a full hour before. I confessed that it was my fault the response team had never been dispatched. He thanked me, hung up and promptly reported me.

When I returned to base the next morning, my supervisor called me in and, almost apologetically, gave me a letter of counseling "in the drawer." You can bet I watched my lights like a hawk from then on and the letter never saw the light of day. Nevertheless, the entire situation left a bad taste in my mouth and solidified my resolve to escape the missile career field.

My one exposure to a court-martial was as a panel member—the military equivalent of jury duty. I was one of eight other officers selected to decide the fate of a sergeant accused of molesting his then-four-year-old daughter. It was a strange and depressing case. The sergeant had been accused by his now ex-wife of the abuse a couple years earlier. The Office of Special Investigations (OSI) was convinced he was guilty but didn't have enough evidence to charge him at the time. Workers at the base hospital had inadvertently destroyed key rape kit samples taken from an exam of the child which significantly damaged the case.

When the sergeant's security clearance came up for renewal two years later, OSI saw a new opportunity to charge the man. Part of a security clearance review is a personal interview of the subject by government investigators. To conduct the interview, the local OSI brought in an investigator who had a national reputation for eliciting confessions. He questioned the sergeant and, shockingly, secured a signed statement from him confessing to molesting his daughter two years prior. The sergeant was quickly charged, but he then claimed the confession was coerced. My panel would hear the evidence and decide if that was the case.

There are several differences between civilian trials and military court-martials. One of the most interesting is that panel members, unlike jury members, are allowed (unless objected by either legal counsel) to question witnesses directly. And this case raised as many questions as it answered.

The daughter, although still only six years old, was put on the stand by the prosecuting attorney. Even stranger, because she was shy, the judge allowed her babysitter, a young teen, to sit beside her. When asked a question, the little girl would whisper the answer in the babysitter's ear. The babysitter would then state what the little girl had told her. As you can imagine, the daughter provided few details about what had occurred when she was four years old. Both attorneys struggled to frame sexual abuse questions that a six year old could understand. Throughout this interchange, the little girl squirmed, looked around and had trouble focusing on what she was being asked. As panel members, we wished for physical evidence and stronger testimony. Without either, it came down to the credibility of the sergeant's written confession.

The sergeant claimed that the investigator threatened him. He said he was told he wouldn't get his security clearance renewed or be allowed to continue his Air Force career unless he confessed. He also said the investigator lied to him by telling him that since the statute of limitations had run out, he would not be charged with a crime. The Air Force simply wanted him to acknowledge his behavior for the internal record. So, he said, he signed the confession to save his Air Force career.

The investigator claimed under oath that he made no such threats but may have misspoken about the statute of limitations. Turns out, it wasn't too late to charge him. For some reason, the interview wasn't recorded. So, it came down to the sergeant's word against the investigator's.

After deliberating a few hours, we came back with a guilty verdict. The sergeant was sentenced by the judge to reduction in rank, forfeiture of pay and several years of prison time in Leavenworth. I've never been completely at peace with that verdict and have often prayed that we made the right decision. When we left the court building, the sergeant's ex-wife, tears filling her eyes, shook each of our hands and whispered over and over, "Thank you. Thank you. Thank you."

Fortunately, a court-martial conviction wasn't a realistic concern for most crew members. What they feared was having negative comments entered into their official record because of an on-alert mistake. Thankfully, the Air Force does have safeguards for small offences. If they are recorded in the officer's record, usually after a couple of years of exemplary duty, or when an officer moves on to a new assignment, the negative comments are removed. This keeps minor infractions from being forwarded to promotion boards, where even the mildest of negative comments can mean the difference between being selected for the next rank or being passed over.

Also, the core document in an officer's official record rarely records anything but positive accomplishments. The annual officer performance reports (OPRs) are records of an alternate universe where every officer is of exemplary character and spends his or her life doing wonderful deeds for the United States of America. It is a rare OPR that an officer's mother wouldn't love.

OPRs are written by the officer's (the ratee's) immediate supervisor (the rater) and signed off by two officers above that supervisor (additional rater and reviewer). Typically, OPRs are crammed full of over-the-top accomplishments described in flowery adjectives that would make a tabloid writer blush. A well-written OPR is a work of art. Unfortunately, some supervisors are finger painters while others are Van Goghs.

If a young ratee is stuck with a finger painter rater, he's going to need to transition from submitter of inputs to co-writer. Together, a ratee and a rater can create egg salad out of rotten eggs. For example, if Lieutenant Red Riding Hood got lost in the woods on the way to Grandma's house and then was eaten by a wolf in disguise—no problem. They can use that. The OPR bullet would read, "Lt Red Riding Hood, while pro-actively blazing new trails through the battlefield, paused to provide a delicious meal to starving woodland creatures."

One of my early OPRs had this line: "Key contributor to the wing's 'Outstanding' Mission Effectiveness rating on the recent HQ SAC Inspector General (IG) evaluation." Since the bullet doesn't specify my key contribution, I believe it was that I was a member of the wing while the inspection occurred and successfully avoided all contact with SAC evaluators.

Sometimes, though, a young lieutenant hasn't been at the squadron long enough to fill up the required 23 lines of accomplishments. That's when a finger painter supervisor gets lazy. Here is one example from my first OPR at Grand Forks: "In an effort to boost morale of his fellow crew members, Lieutenant Cook volunteered off-duty time to install satellite descramblers at our capsules to increase channel selection." Even mama would wince at that line.

As my career progressed and I learned how to provide better inputs, my OPRs improved. The best OPR lines stratified you in relation to your peers. For instance, an OPR just prior to a lieutenant colonel promotion board, might say, "Top 10% of majors I've known" or "#1 of six majors in division." Those lines are worth a hundred "leadership personified" phrases.

I completed my four years on crew with a few bumps and minor scars, but nothing that followed my career like an unwanted stray dog. The Air Force holds their people to an extremely high standard. So, to survive and be promoted is a special honor. What endures, however, even after retirement, is primarily an officer's reputation among his or her peers. That is the true performance report, not some yellowed paper in a forgotten filing cabinet.

CHAPTER 24

Talking Shop

I was behind schedule. After 18 months of deputy crew duty, I remained in the 447th Strategic Missile Squadron pulling eight alerts a month. A treadmill of career drudgery. Where I needed to be was in "the shop," a desk job promotion to train my fellow crew members. And, not insignificantly, a position where my monthly alert requirements would shrink to two.

Most deputies who excelled were selected for shop duty during their initial nine to twelve months at the wing. I was already six months past my *use by* date and in another six months I would be upgrading to commander. That meant I might end my deputy time with a critical achievement left unchecked on my record.

Like a teenager who hasn't been asked to the prom, I wondered, "What's wrong with me?" After all, I had a strong record and the respect of my fellow crew members. I guessed that my low-key personality wasn't helping me stand out from the pack. Maybe I needed to spend more time at the Officer's Club on Friday afternoons, mingling with my coworkers and laughing loudly at my superiors' jokes.

Whatever the reason, it was discouraging to see classmates from Vandenberg get hired while I watched from the sidelines—a proverbial missileer wallflower. I reminded myself that God was in control. I had to just keep working hard.

Home life was a welcome escape from work frustrations. My two boys were always excited to see me walk through the door. In their minds, I was the doer of mighty deeds. Years later, my youngest son, Benjamin, told me that as a child he thought my job was to climb on top of missiles and fly them around the sky. Beth had no such misconceptions, yet she always made me feel like I could do anything. Even ride a missile. She also believed that God was in control of my life. As proof, she daily prayed that he would rain fire and brimstone down on my supervisors until they repented of their sins and recommended me for a shop job. Not really—well, maybe.

While we awaited heavenly retribution, Beth and I tried to get pregnant again. We hoped for a girl this time. Nothing against males, but I was the oldest of four boys growing up. Eight of my ten cousins were boys, as were my first two children. It was high time I experienced the wonderful world of little girls. As a plus, I might also learn a little about the feminine nature. Beth had always lamented my ignorance in that area. One of her frequent sayings was, "I'm not one of your brothers!" Who knew?

My education was moving forward in other areas. I was in my second year of night classes at the University of North Dakota, pursuing a master's degree in physical education. This choice was more career insurance than the pursuit of a dream. The Air Force expected officers to get a graduate degree before their major's promotion board. The subject didn't really matter. I chose physical education so I could possibly become a college professor if the Air Force didn't work out. In retrospect, I regret not exploring other interests rather than choosing a safe fallback degree.

Near the end of my crew tour, I did briefly pursue a new dream, to become a lawyer. I studied several months for the Law School Admission Test (LSAT), took the exam and scored well. My intent was to apply for the Air Force Funded Legal Education Program (FLEP), which is highly competitive. For the few applicants selected, the Air Force not only covers tuition, but also pays a full-time salary during school. It was the only way I could afford to attend law school, with a stay-at-home wife and three small children. To even apply for FLEP, an officer had to already be accepted at an accredited law school. I applied to, and was accepted by, three schools. One of those even offered me a half-tuition scholarship. Unfortunately, I wasn't selected for FLEP, and regretfully turned down the admission offers. Law was a hard door to close, but I concluded that it wasn't meant to be and moved on.

I qualified for 100 percent graduate school tuition coverage simply by being a missile launch officer. In addition, all books and fees were covered through the Air Force's Minuteman Education Program. This was an exclusive benefit, originally offered as an incentive to recruit new missileers. For everyone else, the Air Force only paid 75 percent graduate tuition. Unsurprisingly, the extra 25 percent didn't bring hordes of eager missileer-wannabes pounding on Strategic Air Command's door.

Despite this benefit, some supervisors had convinced their new deputies to defer taking graduate classes for a year or two. The reasoning was that they needed to first focus on learning their jobs. That logic proved faulty when, a few years later, the Air Force unexpectedly initiated a Reduction in Force (RIF). In reviewing personnel records to determine who would be released, the word was that the RIF board was looking for clear discriminators. They seemed to find one in the area of completed graduate work. There were certainly other criteria considered in RIF decisions.

However, it was obvious from the list of missileers who were let go that a common factor was lack of a progress towards obtaining a graduate degree.

Most of my coworkers were enrolled in the more popular graduate programs offered on base. They took business or public administration classes that were populated with other military members along with a few dependents. As the only missileer preparing for a lucrative post-military career in physical education, I attended classes at the university campus downtown.

A side benefit of this commute was meeting people from the local community. For my entire two and half years of study, I was the only military member in my classes. I was an oddity to my classmates, as they were to me. Most of them had never ventured far from North Dakota. Few knew much about the military or what my job entailed. Still, they were friendly in a polite, surface kind of way. As in other close-knit communities near which I would be stationed, it was difficult to crack their social circle. I sensed that they viewed military people as transients, not worth the emotional investment of friendship.

I happened to be in class the night the first Gulf War kicked off in January of 1991. During a break, my professor turned on the television so we could watch CNN reporting on our force's initial missile strikes. She looked over at me and said, "Don't you need to report to base or something?"

I wanted to say, "Yes, ma'am. At 0300 hours a transport plane is scheduled to whisk me overseas to join my fellow warriors for the second wave pushing into Kuwait."

Instead, I was forced to meekly admit, "No, my job doesn't have a direct impact on this war." It occurred to me that if I ever did get recalled to my job, that's when my professor really needed to worry.

In true Air Force fashion, months later, I and all other active-duty members received National Defense Service Medals for active duty service *during* war time. To paraphrase an old comedian, "I'm proud that during my war service in North Dakota, not one Iraqi soldier made it past Fargo."

There were no awards for my master's program, though. Even as a valued Air Force officer, I couldn't escape the disparagement of my former profession. When I told a friend that I was getting my master's in physical education, he was genuinely shocked. "You can get a graduate degree in P.E.?" he asked. I further floored him by replying that not only could I, but it was also possible to get a *PhD* in P.E.! He stared at me, dumbfounded, as if his brain couldn't grasp such an unimaginable concept. I decided not to further traumatize him by revealing that none of my graduate classes had required darkening a gymnasium door or touching a ball.

Over the years, I've noticed that my fellow P.E. majors, like convicted felons, are reluctant to identify themselves. However, I can spot them every time. While others proudly boast of their degrees ("Mechanical Engineering with a minor in Foreign Relations"), when asked about theirs, my compatriots usually mumble a misleading, "education" and quickly turn conversation to the weather. Even I wasn't immune from this defensiveness. The thought crossed my mind that I had been passed over for a shop job because they had discovered that my undergraduate major was in P.E. Maybe I was just another victim of the academic elites!

Then more bad news. I learned that I was scheduled to pull alert with my squadron commander, the intimidating Lieutenant Colonel Meadows. Regulations required all squadron commanders to be certified crew members. To stay qualified, they had to pull alert from time to time.

I dreaded pulling this alert with my boss. Not only would it be extremely uncomfortable, but I feared making a mistake. A mistake would surely torpedo selection for the shop position. On a more practical level, my commander would expect everything to be done by the book. That meant each action and checklist step would slow us to a miserable slog. Not to mention the awkward social interaction. Imagine spending 24 hours in a small hotel room with your gruff boss. It was an introvert's nightmare.

That morning, despite my boss's friendly demeanor, the 45-minute drive out to our alert site seemed like hours. As anticipated, crew changeover was the slowest I had experienced since Vandenberg training. There was none of the usual gossip and joking around between the crews. As he left, the off-going deputy leaned in and whispered, "You girls have fun, now!"

Fun, it was not. However, our shared 24 hours did allow us to get better acquainted. I learned that the colonel had many human-like qualities and wasn't the robotic Strategic Air Command warrior I had perceived. He learned, I hoped, that although I was a quiet guy, I was also a confident and competent officer. Somehow, I made it through that alert without a major stumble.

To my surprise, a few weeks later, Lieutenant Colonel Meadows recommended me for an instructor shop position. The dreaded alert had actually been a godsend. Another life lesson for me. Soon, I was sitting at my new desk with sharpened pencils and a brighter outlook on life.

The shop was primarily housed in one large room lined with desks. There were no cubicles or large desktop computers to shield me from the gaze of my coworkers or office visitors. This open environment promoted a healthy amount of cross-room banter, typically involving jabs regarding snack choices, new haircuts and favorite sports teams. The intellectual-discourse bar was pretty easy to step over—more locker room than academic office. After the isolation of crew life, I found it a refreshing change.

The desk tops themselves were out of a 1940s newspaper movie. There was a phone, IN and OUT baskets filled with papers, and our essential working tools—a yellow legal pad, post-it notes, highlighter and an assortment of pens. The closest thing to cutting-edge technology was a pair of scissors.

We weren't complete savages in 1991. We actually shared one office computer. When I say *shared*, I mean two computer geeks were allowed to operate the machine while the rest of us could only gaze upon it wistfully. Operate a thermonuclear missile launch system? No problem. Touch our office computer? Sorry—too risky.

The American taxpayer had provided us this wondrous computer for two reasons: to churn out more professional training material, such as crew self-study guides and to create projector slides for the classroom. Previously, to create training material, we would write out our content on a legal pad, then hand it to an administrative support troop. He or she would then type it up and make copies. Even with the computer, that was still the process for daily administrative work such as producing official letters. Requiring everything to be processed on a single computer caused too much of a bottleneck.

Despite the use of a computer, our monthly training day briefing slides were still shown on the manual overhead projector. Transparencies of each slide were created, printed out and placed on the bulb-lit projector by the instructor. Computerized slides simply meant no longer needing to use the typewriter or hand-print text directly onto our transparencies.

Our computer was loaded with a state-of-the-art software program called Harvard Graphics (HG), the great-grandfather of Power Point. What sent shivers of delight up our spines was that HG had the ability to place digitized drawings—called clip art—onto a briefing slide to liven up the dull forest of text.

HG was not a military product, so its picture library consisted primarily of animals, barns, musical instruments and generic office people hunkered over sets of blueprints. Undeterred, our shop supervisor made a policy that each briefing slide would have a picture on it. The Air Force had paid good money for HG and darn it—we were gonna get a return on that investment.

Thus, our training slide on Security Situation 6 response might include a drawing of a cow in the corner. Another slide on prepping a missile for launch might be adorned with a group of business people having coffee. At first, we made an effort to place pictures which had some connection, however tenuous, to our subject. But, by slide 48 in a larger briefing, most instructors were just happy to slap a speedboat picture in the corner and be done with it.

As a former teacher, the shop felt like home. I enjoyed writing lessons again and answering questions in class. I felt good about helping my fellow missileers, especially the new ones fresh from Vandenberg.

Another bonus was reconnecting with friends from officer training and Vandenberg who had been assigned to other squadrons. Despite previous bonding experiences, our work lives seldom intersected and we had drifted apart socially. Mitch Catanzaro, my officer training roommate, now worked in the evaluator shop next door, so I saw him several times a week.

Although Mitch wasn't a big sports guy like me, he enjoyed boxing. One night he invited a group of us over to watch the undefeated Mike Tyson's World Heavyweight Championship title defense live via satellite from Japan. Tyson was expected to make quick work of his unknown and underwhelming opponent, Buster Douglas. However, Douglas fought the fight of his life and knocked Iron Mike out in the eighth round. As Tyson was counted out, we all shouted and high-fived each other, forgetting for a moment that we were stuck up in the Great White North, hundreds of miles from our previous lives.

But, like most jobs in the military, it soon came time to move on. After nine months I was required to leave the shop and begin my upgrade training to become a crew commander. That involved selecting a deputy from my former squadron to take the practice rides and certification evaluation with me. It was the only time during a crew member's tour when you are allowed to pick a crew partner. It was a big decision and could make the difference between passing and failing.

I asked Dex Ferrell to support my upgrade. He agreed, although it meant a lot of extra work for him—and no personal benefit. Dex was smart, eternally calm, and when under stress would respond by simply quietly giggling. I knew he'd handle the evaluation pressure well and keep me out of trouble.

My penance for giving him, as sarcastic crew members called it, "another opportunity to excel," was agreeing to be a groomsman at his wedding. He was marrying a local Grand Forks girl at a downtown church. Sure. A small price to pay.

Since the male members of the wedding party were all missile officers, Dex wanted everyone to wear his service dress uniforms. Service dress includes coat, bowtie, cummerbund and medals, the Air Force equivalent of a tuxedo. Although it was June, I didn't mind so much until I arrived at the church and realized it had no air conditioning. My previous history of fainting in hot churches had me concerned.

Despite some light-headed moments, I made it through the ceremony without being dragged out by my heels. Although in a full sweat, I was still coherent enough to join in the military tradition of providing a tunnel of raised swords for the bride and groom to exit through.

Back at base, our practice rides went smoothly. My biggest adjustment was sitting in the unfamiliar commander's chair and allowing Dex to sift through all the missile prints and lights which were only at the status console. Delegating what I previously controlled myself was difficult, but that's part of leadership—trusting your people. I realized that having less console concerns in the commander's seat helped me to think through future decisions and keep the bigger picture in mind.

We sailed through the evaluation with no major errors and were awarded Outstanding Performer status. It was my third, which qualified me for the 20th Air Force Crew Excellence Award. My fledgling career was going well, but I was sad to leave the shop. Becoming a commander meant returning to the 447th and, once again, pulling eight alerts a month. That was fine for the near-term, but I was determined to return to shop duty as soon as possible.

In the meantime, I needed to find new opportunities in the 447th and keep building on my record. Squadron leadership options were few. They were limited to selection as a flight commander or operating the squadron command post (SCP).

A flight commander is in charge of a specific launch control center. There are five of those in each squadron. While crews rotate alerts, the flight commander is always responsible for ensuring his or her capsule is maintained properly. That means it is cleaned regularly, re-supplied and equipment kept functional. Essentially, a flight commander is a kind of subterranean landlord. Not glamorous, but very important to the mission.

Another leadership option for commanders is being certified to work at the squadron command post (SCP). This is the lead capsule of the squadron's five. During a SCP alert, the commander there is in charge of the other four squadron crews, leading combined tests, consolidating information to report up the Air Force chain and ensuring everyone is doing his or her job. SCP capsules have a few additional racks of equipment and, like the other capsules, are capable of monitoring all fifty squadron missiles at once.

Yet, despite the weapon firepower under a crew commander's responsibility, when it comes to personnel, he or she only supervises one person—the deputy. By contrast, a captain in a security forces or civil engineer squadron may supervise 20 or 30 people, many of them first-term airmen. A missileer may not get such a leadership opportunity for ten years until he or she makes lieutenant colonel. However, one underling was better than none and I was happy to help mentor my new deputy.

CHAPTER 25

It's Not the Blast
That Will Kill You

One of the benefits of being a crew commander is pulling the capsule's overnight shift. Typically, at that time there is not much going on. By early evening, most of the missile site maintenance, wing-wide communications exercises and required tests are wrapped up. Things are quiet and a crew commander has time to watch a little television, read, or catch up on paperwork.

Of course, staying not only awake, but alert, from midnight until 6:00 a.m. can be a challenge. The low lights and steady hum of the air conditioning unit are more conducive to napping than work. As a deputy, I knew of a certain commander who would wrap himself in a blanket, put his feet up on the console and lean back in his chair for hours at a time. He was awake—barely—relying on capsule alarms and the occasional rat-a-tat-tat of a printer to shake him out of his bleary-eyed stupor.

Some industrious commanders came up with creative ways to avoid disturbing their reclining, mummy-like state. The capsule was always cold, and once snuggled up, a missileer was not eager to move.

I knew of one officer who took this attitude to an extreme. For every alert he packed a pair of binoculars and a long stick. As he sat bundled up on his late night shift an inevitable alarm would go off and the printer would spit out updated missile status. Unfortunately, the printer was at the status console, which would typically require him to shed his cocoon and amble over to read the print-out. On stormy nights when the launch facilities were experiencing multiple power changeovers, alarms might be going off every few minutes. That's a lot of getting up and down. So, something obviously had to be done about that. Over time, he perfected his labor-saving system.

When an alarm rang, he would use a long stick to hit the ALARM RESET button, thus avoiding the exertion of leaning forward. Because whatever print had just emerged from the status console was still partially hidden by the cover, he would then hit another button on the command console generating a follow-on error print, pushing the one he wanted to read out into the open. Then, he would peer through his binoculars and read the print which was about 25 feet away. If it wasn't one that required action, he laid his head back and resumed whatever stream of semi-conscious thoughts he'd been engaged in. I had to admire such creative laziness.

You might ask if any of these commanders ever fell asleep. Who can say? It would be easy enough to nod off momentarily. However, the frequent alarms and multiple loud communications printers sounding off would make it impossible to doze through a nuclear war.

I usually spent my late-night shifts reading or doing graduate school assignments. I don't know who paid for it, but every month a box of brand-new paperback books, primarily novels, would be delivered to the capsule. We accumulated quite an underground library, but most crew members preferred to bring their own reading material from home.

When I first joined crew in 1990 there was a small television set hanging from the capsule ceiling which was controlled by the security troops topside. Whatever they were watching was piped down to our screen. One of their favorite programs was this reality show (a new concept then) called *Cops*. Unbelievably, that program was continuously on air up until recently.

Before the wing bought the capsules satellite dishes, the local television stations we could reach with our topside antenna would sign off around 2:00 a.m. Those last bleary-eyed, television-free hours before waking up the deputy were the most challenging. To bridge the gap between antenna and satellite television, videocassette recorders (VCRs) were installed in all the capsules. Now we could watch our own movies without negotiating programming with the topside security personnel.

If you desired a late dinner or an early breakfast, you placed an order via intercom with the topside cook. Typically, these novices were barely out of their teens, most on their first Air Force assignments. To say these young people were not the most motivated individuals would be a gross understatement. Many had been lured to military service by flashy recruiting videos depicting fighter jets, dimly lit operations centers and camouflaged special force troops parachuting into the night sky. It must have been deflating to have envisioned that life and then find that your wartime contribution would consist of fixing toasted cheese sandwiches in the middle of North Dakota farmland. There weren't any medals for wounds sustained while slicing tomatoes.

Sadly for us, most of these airmen weren't highly proficient in the culinary arts. The joke was that their official job title should be "microwave heat technician." Our typical menu consisted of grilled burgers, cold sandwiches and entrees in foil packs which were pre-made for being warmed up. I doubt there were any cookbooks or recipe card files on site.

If books, television or food didn't keep you occupied on graveyard shift, you could always get in a workout. Many capsules had stationary bicycles and our space offered a pseudo-walking/jogging track circling the row of inner equipment racks. Only 88 short laps and you had your two miles in. If you were more the sporting type, there were capsules with nice putting greens installed. One even had a helpful map diagraming a nine-hole putt-putt course you could play.

The one task that did keep everyone alert was performing the hold off command. Required every six hours, this consisted solely of resetting a timer which, if left to its own devices, would count down to zero, allowing the capsule's missiles to accept "enable" and "launch" commands from an overhead military airborne command center. With the proper codes, the airborne controllers could launch your missiles. In time of war, this was an automated alternate way the Air Force could still execute the mission if the underground capsules and crews were incapacitated (translation—blown up, injured or dead from a Soviet first strike).

To ensure that this critical six-hour timer reset was not forgotten, the timer set off an alarm ten minutes before expiration, then a final warning at two minutes. This occurred in all five capsules in a squadron. That meant there were at least five missileers in five different locations who had the opportunity to hear the alarm, see the prints and reset the squadron timer.

If all these safeguards failed, the next printout a missileer saw (and never wanted to see) was a string of codes from each of the missiles essentially saying, *I'm ready to be launched via aircraft.* This was never supposed to happen but if it did, all five capsule crews were in for a bad week.

The squadron command post (SCP) capsule always took the lead on resetting the hold off timer. At the ten-minute mark, the SCP crew member would call up the other capsules on a party line and announce, "It's time for the hold off. I've got it. Watch for proper indications." After sending the command, it was everyone's responsibility to ensure that their flight of ten missiles saw the command and accepted the timer reset.

At the 321st Strategic Missile Wing, this action was performed without fail four times every 24 hours, 365 days a year, year after year, decade after decade. Except once—that I'm aware of.

One night shift in my squadron, all five crew commanders missed the ten-minute warning. *And then* missed the two-minute warning! By the grace of God, I was not on alert. When the horrified crews realized their error, they quickly reset the timer but it was too late. All fifty missiles were open to outside commands for a few excruciating minutes. All five crews were awarded reprimands for their personnel files, temporarily de-certified and assigned additional training. That included the crew members who were in bed at the time and asleep when the screw up happened.

Were the Minuteman missiles ever in danger of being launched by a sinister force? I'd say no. There weren't any properly equipped military airborne command centers in the area. Even if there were, they would not have had the legitimate orders or even the required codes to unlock the missile computers. Of course, that didn't matter. The capsule crews had failed to take a basic required action to safeguard their sole control of the missiles. To err is human; to forgive was not Strategic Air Command policy.

Years later, I was watching the popular network series, *Lost*, about survivors of a plane crash on a strange tropical island. They discovered an underground operations center, dubbed "the hatch." Inside lived a slightly traumatized man, also an unwilling prisoner of the island, who had been ordered to sit at this particular console and reset a countdown timer every 108 minutes. He didn't know what would happen if he let the timer expire but was too afraid to find out. It was an interesting concept that was familiar enough for me to wonder if one of the scriptwriters was a former missileer.

Although the Air Force trained crew members to engage in nuclear warfare, it did little to prepare us for the potential aftermath. If they provided us any training on post-nuclear war survival, I don't recall it. Not that we were clamoring for such training. Most of us believed the risk of nuclear war was small. Even smaller were the odds that we would make it through such a missile exchange and require guidance on how to survive as Mel Gibson–like road warriors in a post-apocalyptic world. Such a war would be an unprecedented and catastrophic event from which the Air Force, what was left of it, would have little resources to help us recover.

For starters, we assumed that Grand Forks Air Force Base, as well as launch control centers and missile silos would be targeted by the Soviets in a first strike. Even if we did get our missiles launched, the United States had no system in place to defend us from the enemy missiles headed our way. Chances were, we would die not only in a direct hit, but also a near miss. As the old saying goes, "Close only matters in atom bombs and horseshoes." Even more vulnerable were our families back home, totally exposed above ground.

All I knew was that there were meals ready to eat (MREs) stored under the capsule which might keep me and my crew partner alive for a while. There was also a 750-gallon tank of emergency water under the floor, but I can't recall how we were supposed to access it. The fresh air in the capsule would not last that long and eventually, we would be required to make our way to the surface. If the tunnel junction outside the blast door had collapsed, our only escape was a hatch inside the capsule, connected to a tunnel. We had never been allowed in this tunnel for good reason: it was full of sand.

The escape procedure called for the crew members to open the hatch and allow the sand filling the 60-foot slanted tunnel to drain directly into the capsule. Afterwards, the crew would take a small shovel and climb up inside the tunnel, making their way to where it ended, about five feet below the surface. From there, the crew members would dig their way to the surface, then emerge into whatever above-ground nightmare was there to meet them. That's where our guidance ended. After that we were on your own. No vehicle left for us to drive, no base to which we could return to and no way of knowing where we might report. Maybe that was a scenario the Air Force didn't want us to ponder.

In keeping with the typical missileer's dark humor, several jokes made the rounds about this escape tunnel plan. One was that some math whiz had calculated that the volume of sand in the escape tunnel was greater than the volume of the capsule, meaning that when the escape hatch was opened the two crew members would drown in a sand avalanche.

Another version was that the sand had been inside the leaky tunnel for so many years that it had petrified and upon opening the hatch the crew would be staring at solid rock. Then there was the joke that the civil engineers, not knowing about the escape tunnel, had extended the parking lot pavement over that section of ground, again giving the crew a solid surface to bust through.

So, the low risk of performing our war time mission combined with the pessimism about our ultimate survival meant we spent little time contemplating this scenario. However, I do remember once thinking that if the Soviets ended up controlling the world, the United States was essentially reduced to a third world country, and all my loved ones were gone, I may not want to survive.

Sometimes an enthusiastic young missileer would wax poetic about how the steel capsule, protected by layers of dirt, was designed to remain intact, even during a nearby nuclear detonation. Invariably, a gnarly veteran would grunt and respond, "It ain't the blast that'll kill you, it's the 40-foot fall to the bottom of the crater that nuke explosion will make." Maybe that's better than facing a post-apocalyptic world.

CHAPTER 26

Grooving to the Groobers

If the average citizen were asked to describe the missile crew force in a few words, "artsy" or "barrel of laughs" probably wouldn't spring to mind. And who could blame them? As a group, missileers presented a picture of disciplined, boring, blue-suited uniformity. Yet, closer examination would reveal a good many crew members with quirky personalities, creative minds and a sharp wit rivaling members of any civic arts community.

Case in point, the legendary Groobers. In 1975, this quartet of singing, yet unsung, missileers was birthed at F.E. Warren Air Force Base in Cheyenne, Wyoming. The Groobers burst into fleeting northern tier fame by writing and recording missile crew parodies to well-known folk, doo-wop and country songs. Armed with a banjo, acoustic guitar and beautiful four-part harmonies, these crew dogs were the hit of the mid-seventies SAC dinner circuit.

To truly appreciate the comedy gold of the Groobers lyrics, you had to be a missileer yourself. Yet even outsiders could appreciate the humor, delivered in Kingston Trio–mocking false-earnestness. Granted, a few of their song lyrics, although given a pass fifty years ago, would not be socially acceptable humor today.

A sampling of their more family-friendly hits includes *There Are No Missile Men Down in Hell* and *The Crew that Never Returned*. Another song, *Nothing's Too Good for the Missile Men* had the following lyrics:

> *Chorus:*
> Nothing's too good for the missile men and nothing is just what we get.
> The pilots get all the gravy, the missile men get all the grit.
>
> *Last verse:*
> I shinnied the pole up to Heaven, oh listen to what I do tell
> When I saw the SAC sign on the pearly gates, I thought I was surely in Hell.
> St. Peter was watching me struggle, he threw back his head and he laughed
> He said everyone else rides the elevator, the missile men still get the shaft.

Fifteen years later, cassette versions of their album were still passed among the crew force like bootleg copies of a lost Beatles album. Of course, the Groobers didn't have much competition in the narrow music category of Nuclear Missile Folk Music.

Although Grand Forks did not produce any Groobers tribute bands, it did offer its share of witty and artistic crew members. Many of these amateur entertainers preferred displaying their talents in more private venues. One of these venues was a green logbook which was found in almost every launch capsule. The logs had originally been made available so crew members could pen helpful notes for other crews following them on alert. These notes might be scintillating entries such as "Remember to jiggle the toilet lever. If not, the water tends to run continuously. Let's not waste taxpayer money on high water bills!"

Eventually, crew members tired of such drudgery and began using log entries to upbraid other crews who had not cleaned up after themselves, or as a platform for venting frustrations with crew life in general. Soon, the logbook was re-christened *the gripe book* and other less politically correct monikers.

Bored missileers began expanding logbook entries to display their artwork, draw cartoon strips skewering heavy-handed supervisors, or to record stream of consciousness thoughts for the entertainment of future readers. By the time I was assigned to Grand Forks, the gripe book had become required reading on alert. It was a 1990s version of Twitter, Facebook and Pinterest all wrapped into one.

Despite the insults hurled both with humor and without, there were unspoken boundaries. No one derided another crew member's spouse, kids or religion. Politics was fair game though, as were opinions on a person's dating choices.

Although not endorsing their use, senior wing officers were well aware of these logs. Once women were integrated into the crew force, our leadership became even more concerned. What if a crew member's insulting entry was reported by the subject as workplace harassment or conduct unbecoming an officer? Would their own careers be in jeopardy for allowing these logs in the capsule? Other wing leaders saw the practice as a needed outlet for frustrated crew members and were happy to tolerate a "don't ask, don't tell" situation.

Every so often, a squadron commander would receive a complaint and then demand that all flight commanders purge their capsules of these books. The flight commanders would comply, but eventually another gripe book would be started. Most gripe books were hidden in spare capsule equipment drawers to guard against discovery during a no-notice evaluator or leadership visit. When the books were ultimately removed, many flight commanders took them home as souvenirs. They thus preserved what I consider an important historical artifact of crew life.

During a later assignment I was able to obtain one of these books which had been spirited out of Foxtrot-Zero in 1989. Flipping through it, I was overjoyed to discover that it contained some of the legendary artwork of one missileer who created a cartoon series depicting the launch capsule as a kind of subterranean, Starship *Enterprise*. His version was dubbed "The Sub-Prairie Ballistic Missile Cruiser (SS-SPBMC)." This launch capsule/submarine roamed the earth below North Dakota tugging along its missile silos connected via cables to the mothership like a squid's trailing tentacles. Later versions pictured the capsule being carried via air balloon over Russia to drop its missiles. Another cartoon depicted the capsule being hurled towards Russia by a giant wooden catapult from King Arthur days.

To truly appreciate a gripe book entry, you need to not only be a missileer, but to also see the artwork accompanying the verbiage. That said, here is sampling from the Foxtrot-Zero gripe book covering April 1987 to April 1989. Spoofing the required security classification markings on formal SAC documents, someone labeled the inside cover with "UNCLASS (No class at all)."

One page described the nine-hole mini-golf course laid out in the capsule:

> 1st Hole: Tee off a Shock Isolator #4. Hole is between chair rails even with Alarm Monitor Rack. Par 2. Easy shot if you drive first shot between rails. Could be tough to chip 2nd shot over rail if you don't.
> 2nd Hole: Tee off next to support beam by PDG. Watch out. Dog leg left to hole by Shock Isolator #2. Par 3. Like indoor soccer, bank shots are legal. Under equipment racks are out of bounds.

An entry from a crew dog nicknamed "Crash," giving advice on writing annual officer evaluation report (OER) bullets:

> For those of you having trouble writing OERS I'd like to give you a Crash course in hyperbole. The following is OER example number 162:
> [Actual event: 2nd Lt Smith got sunburned while waterskiing and sprayed Solarcain on affected area.]
> OER version of event: 2nd Lt Smith walks on water and heals the sick!

Another entry from missileer upset after being "burned" as the back-up and having to take an alert for another crew member who couldn't go:

> I came out here on a split because my back-up got burned by a wimp who bruised his arm. I find it inconceivable that I could pull alert for 3 and a half months with casts on both arms, at different times of course, and a guy with a bandage and low threshold of pain tolerance gets Duty Not including Alert (DNIA) for five days. We need some more "real men" on crew. Enough with the Quiche Eaters. Anyway, this site is a dump (rant continues at the flight commander for low supplies and broken items).

On August 25, 1987, this entry listing Murphy's Laws:

Murphy was a missileer.
1. Anything that can go wrong, will go wrong. And an evaluator will observe it.
2. No one's life, liberty or property are safe with the Inspector General team on base.
3. Anything Job Control tries to fix will take longer and cost more than you think.
4. Any tool dropped while repairing a Titan missile will cause a nuclear detonation.
5. If more than one person is responsible for a miscalculation, the crew commander will be at fault.

Random October 10, 1987 entry:

Linda Blair (of Exorcist fame) would make a great deputy crew commander for trainer rides. She could do a 360-degree scan of the capsule in a second. Her smell would keep the evaluators away and her projectile vomiting could put out fires.

Entry which begins with four dots spaced like four corners of a square:

Existence test: Connect the dots.
If your answer looks like a square, then you thought. Therefore, you are. So at the time of the test, you did exist. You qualify to pull alerts. However, if you re-take the test in the future and fail, contact Wing Command Post and tell them you no longer think. Therefore, you are not. You will be relieved immediately and be reassigned to Services as a cook.

Next entry by another missileer:

Well, my first alert-underground in North Dakota. To be honest, I'm not impressed. What I want to know is where's the travel, where's the pay, where's the adventure? One of these days I'm gonna take my recruiter and put him in an LF (on top of a minuteman III) and let him become the first Air Force Missile Pilot.

A December 17, 1987, entry, spreading Christmas cheer:

I think it's time we got a new communications system down here. I love it when the SLFCS is Ker-chunking, the SACDINs buzzing, and flashing, AFSAT is beeping, and PAS is warbling. How about one that has an air horn and strobe lights? Or maybe one that emits sounds like the fingernails on a chalkboard? Better yet, an alarm that repeats the theme of Gilligan's Isle. There must be an Obnoxious Noise Department somewhere in SAC. They're damn good at their work.

Suggested motto for crew force in 1988:

We are the unwilling, working for the unqualified, to do the unnecessary, for the ungrateful.

Response by flight commander to an entry by a previous crew pulling alert at his capsule:

Crew's gripe book entry: Try something novel—get a can opener for the site.

Flight commander's gripe book response: The acquisition committee here at F-0 will be holding their quarterly meeting in October to discuss LCC purchases. Rest assured your request for a can opener will be considered. However, you failed to mention what type of can opener you require. Is it the standard hole punch/bottle cap opener or the advance hand-operated can lid remover? We have to keep our orders specific so the accounting department can disburse our assets properly. If the committee approves spending for your can opener, then it must appear before the budget committee for final approval. If funds are allocated, (as long as contract bidding goes smoothly) we should be able to have the can opener on site as early as June of 1988. Of course, you could always withdraw a buck-fifty out of your mattress and purchase one tomorrow at Target. You could then carry it in your flight bag out to alert for your own personal use. But I know how tight money is these days.

Entry with NUDET (nuclear detonation) lyrics, to the tune of "New York, New York":

> Start turning the keys
> They're leaving today
> I'm gonna be a part of it, NUDET, NUDET

> These sorties are loosed
> They're all "Missile Away"
> We'll make a brand-new start of it, NUDET, NUDET

> Chorus:
> I wanna shake up, those commies who give us trouble
> And find I'm king of the hole, top of the rubble

> Those vagabond birds
> They're longing to stray
> I want to be re-targeting, NUDET, NUDET

When I wasn't on alert enjoying gripe book entries, I performed other additional duty responsibilities. One of those was participating in base exercises in my role of START escort. The Strategic Arms Reduction Treaty (START) was a treaty between the United States and the Soviet Union. It was signed in July 1991 but wasn't entered into force until 1994. The treaty barred each signatory from fielding more than 6,000 nuclear warheads on top of a combined 1,600 ICBMs and bombers. To enforce this treaty, contingents from each country were allowed to visit the other's bases and verify the treaty was being complied with. As a START escort I was one of a team of wing officers and enlisted members who would assist our senior leadership by accompanying the Soviet team on these visits. Our escort role was not to engage directly with the Russians, but to observe and keep them corralled while they toured the base. If they tried to go somewhere they weren't allowed, or take something they weren't supposed to take, we were there to report that to our superiors. Growing up as the eldest of four brothers, I was an expert in tattling and therefore, perfect for this job.

Since the treaty wasn't in force yet, we held base exercises with a team of airmen taking on the role of visiting Soviets. To test our alertness, they would attempt to surreptitiously pocket alert schedules left out on tables or demand to look inside doors to prohibited rooms. For instance, if a Russian insisted on viewing the inside a closet, I was to report him to a senior treaty official on the United States team. That person would theoretically hustle over and say, "Now Vladimir, you know that this broom closet is not large enough to hide a Minuteman III warhead. Thus, in accordance with the treaty, you do not have a right to take a peek."

In addition to escorting the Russians around base, we were also required to bus the Soviets out to a pre-determined launch facility where we would open up the silo and the missile re-entry shroud. This allowed the Russians to peer down at the Minuteman III and verify there were only the permissible three warheads, not five or six. To guard against deception, the Russians would carry instruments which gave them the exact geodetic coordinates of each launch facility, ensuring they were where we said they were. I guess *trust but verify* went both ways.

The strangest aspect of the START exercise was escorting the simulated Russians to the Base Exchange. We were told, a shopping trip to the installation's retail store was a highly anticipated benefit for our foreign visitors. I couldn't fathom what merchandise was so alluring in our small, military-themed version of JC Penny's. But then again, I didn't know what material goods were *not* available in Russia. I heard that blue jeans would definitely be a hot item on their shopping list.

Years later, while stationed at Patrick Air Force Base in Florida, I discovered this phenomenon was not exclusive to our Soviet friends. I was helping to escort a group of about 40 military officers from several foreign countries who were on a two-week trip in the United States, visiting various military bases. When they arrived at our Florida base, we did our best to arrange tours showcasing our nation's space launch mission. Near the end of their last day, we were up at Kennedy Space Center and told them we only had a couple hours left. We had arranged to take them to space launch complex (SLC) 39 so they could see the space shuttle up close—a rare opportunity even for NASA employees.

The catch was that if we stopped at SLC-39, there would not be enough time to take them by the Patrick Air Force Base Exchange (BX) to shop. Upon given this choice, the foreign officers immediately voted to bypass the space shuttle and proceed directly to the BX. I was dumbfounded. Yet, an hour later, they were excitedly pushing shopping carts overflowing with boots, jeans, designer t-shirts, coats and anything else that was distinctly American. I guess we don't appreciate the abundance of material goods available to us here.

Although START exercises, gripe books, intramural sports and other diversions helped pass the time, as I approached the end of my crew tour, I was anxious to move on. I had lived almost four years in our base house, the longest I had lived in any home my entire life. It seemed like forever, and I was never more ready for a change in scenery.

CHAPTER 27

Jail Break

As my four years on crew came to a close, so did my time as a father of three. This arrival wasn't planned. Beth and I already had two boys and a darling little girl. We had decided three offspring was about our limit due to our modest income and matching energy levels. We thought we had successfully shut down operations in the Cook baby-making factory. Yet, without consulting with us, God made a unilateral decision to turn the machinery back on. So, in my final summer at Grand Forks, we learned that we were, once again, pregnant.

Upon sharing the news with our friends, the reaction was noticeably different from our previous announcements. Responses to the first three pregnancies were "Oh, how wonderful!" For this one we simply got the "Oh...," often accompanied by a look that said, "You know how to prevent these things, right?"

Even Beth's doctor immediately asked her, "Do you want to keep this one?" She was shocked, and so was I, that it was even a question. Of course, we did! And over 27 years later, we can't imagine our family without the bubbly personality of Lindsay Joy. Her sister has certainly benefited from having a fellow warrior in the on-going Resistance against older-brother oppression.

My expanding family made me even more anxious to expand my Air Force career beyond missile duty and North Dakota. As the end of my four-year crew commitment neared, I noted similar unrest among my fellow crew members. Almost to a person, those a few months ahead of me were working follow-on assignments outside the 18XX (missile operations) career field.

Prior to 1993, young officers did not have much say in their next assignment. They were required to fill out a "dream sheet" conveying long-term career goals and listing up to three desired assignments in order of priority. The forms were turned into local wing leadership who added their own recommendations based on their expertise and the officer's duty performance.

The form, along with the officer's annual performance reports and other paperwork was forwarded to the Air Force Military Personnel Center (MPC) in Texas. There, behind closed doors, nameless and faceless assignment experts made the job matches. It was a well-known truth in the command that MPC is where lieutenants' dreams went to die.

Many dream sheets elicited a *you're dreaming!* type of response. There were too few great jobs that needed to be filled and too many lousy ones that, unfortunately, someone had to take. This was especially true in the missile career field where they were reluctant to allow crew members to leave after the command had already invested four years into their training and development.

Yet mercy shined down on the poor missileers of 1993. Inexplicably, perhaps in some temporary bout of insanity, MPC instituted a new assignment process. Now all open Air Force positions were advertised on this new internet thing. Officers seeking an assignment could personally look up potential assignments, and, if the unit wanted them, they could be accepted for the assignment without relying on MPC. This kind of autonomy was unheard of and made the oppressed hordes in missile land almost giddy with delight. The only speed bump on this road to freedom was that a senior commander at the officer's current unit had to agree to the tentative assignment.

I observed the feverish glee of my fellow crew members as they worked assignments to Florida, California, Nevada, Colorado, Europe and other magical lands with sunlight, large cities and an array of cultural and entertainment possibilities. I was anxious to reach the four-months-until-end-of-crew mark when I could start working my own escape.

Many of our senior leaders, most of them career missileers, were concerned by the number of crew members they saw fleeing their chosen career field. They first tried to make the case that cross-training out of missiles would hurt an officer's career. It would mean starting from scratch instead of leveraging the four years of experience and expertise a crew member had just accumulated. That pitch, for the most part, fell on deaf ears. All that crew members could envision gaining from staying in 18XX was a career bouncing around isolated northern tier bases, with maybe one or two furloughs to the Pentagon or Vandenberg in California. Many chose to take their chances in a new field.

One of the more feeble 18XX initiatives to help back-fill open crew positions was offering a second assignment, although shorter, missile crew tour at another base. You would not only continue pulling alerts, but also serve as a senior mentor/instructor to first-tour crew members. I only knew of one guy who bit on this dubious bait. To paraphrase the family truckster car salesman in *National Lampoon's Vacation*, "You say you hate four years of crew duty now, just wait until you do six."

Finally, my time to apply for assignment arrived. I sat down at the one computer terminal dedicated to the open assignment database and began to search. I soon found what I was looking for: an entry-level analyst job in Intelligence. That had been one of my three requested career fields way back when I had applied for Officer Training School. Subsequently, my officer training roommate, Mitch, had urged me in that direction. He had been an imagery analyst as an enlisted sergeant and frequently gushed about how exciting the Intelligence world was. Mitch was now leaving missile crew two months before me and had already worked his own assignment back into that field. I wanted to follow him.

However, since I had no Intelligence background, I would first need several months of initial training at Goodfellow Air Force Base in Texas. I applied for the job opening and was quickly accepted! The system assigned me a training date and MPC was poised to make it all a reality. That is, as soon as I obtained the approval of Colonel Jones, my 321st Operations Group Commander. *No problem*, I thought. No crew member ahead of me had failed to get approval for a cross-train assignment out of missiles. You can see where this is going.

A few weeks after I received my tentative assignment, I received a note stating Colonel Jones wanted to see me. Since I hadn't screwed up recently or performed any deed worthy of a medal presentation, I was concerned. "Concerned" is the politically correct Air Force word for "scared." As in, "I was concerned when I noticed that my aircraft's left engine had just fallen off."

I knew this meeting had to be about my assignment. I made the appointment, but the secretary did not have any additional information on what we were to discuss. I hoped he wanted to personally congratulate me for successfully escaping his chosen career field. I sensed that wasn't it.

My buddy, Gary, had received a similar meeting request, scheduled for the same day. Ominously, he had also just received tentative notice of a non-missiles assignment. For me, anxiety was an occasional hobby. For Gary, it was a way of life.

Gary was the Woody Allen of the crew force. Everything made him nervous. I still don't know how he endured four years of crew life without incurring multiple heart attacks.

The week before we were to meet with Colonel Jones, Gary was in full panic mode. Each morning, he'd saunter over to my desk in DOT, sweating profusely and jiggling change in his pocket. "So whadda ya think? Think he's gonna deny us our assignments? Huh, huh? Probably? He wouldn't do that, would he? You think he would? What are the chances? Give me a percentage. More than fifty? Oh boy, I'll be so pissed if he ... but he might not, right? I mean, what do you think? That's not right, not right, man. But I'm worrin' for nuthin, probably, I guess, maybe. You agree, right?"

This went on for several days until I was ready to be retained in missiles just to stop having these conversations.

On the appointed day, I entered Colonel Jones' office and closed the door. As he offered me a seat, I searched for signs in his demeanor of what was to come. The signs weren't good. He wore a look of resigned sympathy, much like a doctor who is about to tell a patient that the x-rays have revealed he may want to get his affairs in order.

"Scott," he began. *Uh, oh,* I thought. *A personal touch, not even using my rank.*

"Last week, I received your assignment request for my approval and unfortunately, I can't sign it." *I hope that means a bad case of carpel tunnel syndrome or an unanticipated pen shortage.*

"I wish I could have signed it. I really do. You've done a great job here but we've had so many crew members opting out of follow-on 18XX assignments that we can't fill our missile wing openings for junior officers."

This can't be happening. All I could manage was a weak, "Yes, sir."

"Bottom line, Scott, I need to stop the bleeding. *By stabbing me??* Too many crew members are leaving the career field."

Is that a surprise to anyone? "Then, what are my options, sir?"

"Well, we have some great follow-on two-year assignments here at the wing. You could be an EWO instructor, an EWO planner, or even work in the Codes Division if you wanted. They're all top jobs to have on your resume. They'll set you up nice for your eventual majors board."

I nodded with a glazed stare. *I don't care about making major right now. I can't take another year in North Dakota.* "Sir, are there missile jobs I could apply for outside of the wing?"

"Well, there are a few Strategic Command headquarters positions at Offutt AFB." *Omaha? As in "Nebraska"? No thanks.* "Of course, you can always go to Vandenberg and teach at the school house or work with the test missile shot folks there." *Vandenberg or icebergs? Simple choice for me.*

The colonel leaned forward. "I'm sorry. I know you had your hopes set on Intelligence school. Unfortunately, we all serve according to the needs of the Air Force ... but you take your time. Mull it over and let me..."

"I'd like to go to Vandenberg and teach at the schoolhouse," I blurted out, somewhat startling him. Meeting over.

And so Gary and I became the first two crew members to have the EXIT door shut in their faces. I was crushed. Yet, like many disappointments in life, it takes a few years to truly gain perspective on what seems like a negative event. Five years later I was relieved that I had not been approved for the Intelligence career field. Turns out career progression was difficult and many intelligence assignments entailed long months away from the family. I doubt I would have been as happy as Mitch.

Vandenberg proved to be a breath of fresh air (literally). Our young family could finally enjoy all that California had to offer without the stress of me being a missile school student. We lived in base housing on a beautiful tree-lined street that reminded me of my childhood neighborhood in Hawaii. Soon after moving, my wife gave birth to Lindsay at the base hospital, finally completing our family of six. Life was good.

Work was only a five-minute commute and never once did I need to shovel snow off my driveway. I rediscovered my love of teaching both in the classroom and in the trainer. I felt fulfilled passing on my expertise to young lieutenants preparing for their own first assignments. It was refreshing to have students who actually hung on my every word and were motivated to learn. What a stark contrast to my former teaching job where I dealt with sullen and unmotivated boarding school students.

Although crew life was over for me, I sympathized with my students who were about to begin their own four years in the Great White North. One of my students was delayed in training because her security clearance was taking longer than usual. When we reached the EWO portion of the course, she had to drop out temporarily. She was assigned to another office on base to do administrative work while she waited. They loved her at the new office. This probably was due to the fact that she was a sharp young officer. Another factor may have been that she was also an attractive blonde female officer.

For whatever reason, once she got a taste of Air Force life outside of missiles, she began to have second thoughts about returning to training. I suspect that her new boss and co-workers, hoping to keep her, gave her some bad advice. One morning I learned that she had met with our commander and requested that, regardless of her security clearance outcome, she be released from missile school. She asserted that after some soul-searching, she had concluded that she couldn't, in good conscience, launch nuclear missiles.

Of course, opting out of the 18XX career field on moral grounds was an option we all were given. However, that decision generally concluded with the Air Force revoking your commission and processing you out of the service. That was not what my lieutenant had in mind. She was adamant that she still wanted to remain an Air Force officer. She didn't have an issue with the Air Force launching missiles, she just couldn't do it herself. Then she overplayed her hand by suggesting that maybe they could just leave her in the administrative office she was now in at Vandenberg.

The commander thanked her for her helpful suggestion, but stated

Cook family portrait during the author's assignment as a Vandenberg missile operations instructor. Left to right: Ben, Tori, Brett, wife Beth with Lindsay on her lap, and the author (author's collection).

that if she couldn't fulfill her missile operations commitment, she would be processed out of the Air Force. Soon after digesting that news, the lieutenant searched her soul once again and realized that she could, after all, in good conscience, launch nuclear missiles. A few weeks later her clearance came through and she was back in the trainer with a new student crew partner. She did well the rest of the course and graduated without further incident. I heard later she did eventually get an early release from missile duty and grabbed a sweet job working for NASA.

After three years at Vandenberg, like my lieutenant student, I was finally able to escape the missile career field. By then, missile operations and space operations were both under Air Force Space Command. Now, missileers who wanted to make the Air Force a career were advised to cross-train and get space experience. The downside for junior space operations officers was that they, in turn, were now pressured to take a missile crew tour. Many voluntarily left the military just to avoid that one assignment.

I was encouraged by a fellow instructor to work a space launch assignment at Cape Canaveral Air Force Station like he had just done. Despite the fact that this advice came from the former tiger mascot for Louisiana State University, I took it.

CHAPTER 28

The Cape Crusader

Some say that Florida and North Dakota are not as different as one might think. They are wrong. Florida and North Dakota are both states and both have a fairly flat landscape. That about begins and ends their commonality. Shared characteristics of a missile crew assignment and space launch duty also makes for a short list.

When Strategic Air Command was de-activated at the end of the Cold War, missileers took on the persona of unwanted orphans. They were initially shuffled off to the doorstep of Air Combat Command, a fighter aircraft world which didn't really want them. A couple years later, the missile career field was adopted by Air Force Space Command. It was a better fit than air operations, but still an odd pairing. The space career field was divided into four mission areas: satellite operations, space surveillance, space control and space launch. None of these involved tactical or strategic weapons. I was headed to space launch, the mission most analogous to missile duty.

Arriving at my new duty station, I immediately noted that instead of tall grain silos dotting the countryside, I saw tall mobile service towers and rockets on launch pads. It was exciting to begin work at such a historic base where launches weren't simulated.

Cape Canaveral Air Force Station (as it was called then) sits on the central east coast of Florida. The 1996 version boasted over 15,000 acres, offering a 10,000-foot runway, dozens of processing facilities and 48 launch pads, most of which were test sites abandoned after fulfilling their use in the 1950s and 1960s. Ironically, many of them had been utilized to test early versions of intercontinental ballistic missiles, including the Minuteman. Three complexes were still active for space launches, supporting the Titan IV, Atlas II and Delta II launch vehicles. In the mid–90s, these three stalwarts combined for approximately 30 launches a year. That seems like a busy schedule until you learn that in 1960, there were over 200 launches from the Cape.

Immediately to the west of this busy installation is National Aeronautics and Space Administration's (NASA) Kennedy Space Center (KSC). It boasted two launch pads, built for the Apollo moon program, but during

172

my tenure used for space shuttle missions. A causeway over the Banana River connected my base to KSC. Our Air Force wing also controlled most of the weather instrumentation, radars, cameras, and other range equipment supporting NASA launches. In fact, if a space shuttle veered off course towards civilian populated areas and needed to be destroyed, an Air Force safety expert had that heavy burden.

To the south of Cape Canaveral Air Force Station were cruise ship ports and the surf shops and hotels lining Cocoa Beach. However, facing east from the base, one saw only miles of uninhabited Atlantic Ocean. The ability to immediately launch over water was one of the primary reasons the Cape was chosen to launch these huge rockets. When rocket stages burned out in flight, they fell into the ocean and sank. Another reason for a large ocean space.

My squadron was housed in a temporary building at Launch Complex-36, home of the Atlas II. I discovered that many of my fellow officers were, like me, former missileers. In fact, on the space launch maintenance side, most of the enlisted troops had also just left missile assignments. We all soon realized that while we had gained sunshine and a vibrant operations environment, we had also lost much of the responsibility we had previously as missile officers.

Launching above-ground rockets, carrying multi-million-dollar satellites, was a much more complicated and risk-adverse process than launching Minuteman IIIs. It required bigger and more powerful rockets than the Minuteman (not counting the warheads, of course).

Minuteman missiles needed to be launched quickly before they themselves were destroyed. So, they were designed as a much simpler rocket. Their solid propellant eliminated the requirement for pre-launch fueling. Once launched, they followed a fairly simple ballistic trajectory towards their target. This was much easier than placing a satellite in a specific place in a specific orbit thousands of miles into space. If a Minuteman missile failed to hit its target, others in the arsenal could be reassigned to do the job. But, if an Atlas II malfunctioned and the satellite didn't reach its intended orbit, millions of dollars were simply gone. A replacement satellite might not be available for launch until many years later. The government had one shot and no insurance to cover a failure.

Ironically, the Atlas and Titan launch vehicles had begun their operational lives as strategic missiles. In the early 1960s, variants of both would be used to carry the nation's early astronauts into space. John Glenn completed the first U.S. earth orbit in an Atlas D. A few years later, a Titan variant carried the two-man astronaut crews of the Gemini program preparing for the Apollo moon shots.

Across the river from our installation, NASA's Kennedy Space Center cast a long shadow. Although the Air Force was launching a couple rockets a month at Cape Canaveral Air Force Station, the fewer, more spectacular space shuttle launches received most of the media and tourist attention. Making it even harder to differentiate between the Air Force's role in space and NASA's was the fact that the early NASA human spaceflight missions all originated from our base. The first U.S. satellite and all the Mercury and Gemini missions were launched on our side of the river. That was true of the initial Apollo program tests, including the 1967 pad fire that took the lives of the three astronauts.

It was exciting to go for a lunch run and jog by the old launch pads where so much history was made. It was thrilling to have a front seat to space shuttle launches as those majestic birds tore off the pad, climbing near our squadron building and out over the ocean. I also got a kick out of tourists in town mistaking me for an astronaut because of my blue flight suit. I always corrected them, but most demanded a picture anyway. As one of them said, "The folks back home won't know the difference." Yet, it was a little frustrating to learn that the average citizen didn't know that there was any space activity in Florida outside of NASA.

What was even more frustrating was discovering that although I was being certified as a space launch crew commander, in fact, I had little responsibility on launch day. The key countdown actions and all crucial monitoring of launch vehicle systems were accomplished by seasoned contractor engineers. The Atlas II was launched by Lockheed-Martin engineers. Their office building was next to ours at complex-36, but worlds apart in focus. These contractors, hired by the Air Force, controlled all major decisions about the processing and launching of the Atlas II. Junior officers like me were mainly present to facilitate communication between Lockheed-Martin and the Air Force.

Our wing was responsible for some crucial areas, including the Eastern Range instrumentation that tracked the launch vehicles, creating the launch schedule, enforcing safety practices, and providing security. We also owned the land. So, Lockheed-Martin and the other launch contractors were required to consult with the Air Force on a number of key issues.

Yet, the primary reason Lockheed-Martin answered to the Air Force and U.S. government was because they were launching military satellites. So, they were contractually required to give us oversight of any maintenance, equipment and software issues which might impact the success of a launch. For this "looking over the shoulder" role, the Air Force launch squadrons employed enlisted maintenance troops to observe the contractors perform key tasks out on the pad. The Air Force also employed their own engineers who attended contractor technical meetings to give the Air Force an independent assessment of any concern areas.

That left us operators. Most of us were not engineers. We helped facilitate interaction between the contractors and the wing, but on launch day, were not given authority to push any buttons or turn any keys to launch a rocket. Unlike missiles, these launch missions demanded people with a technical background and years of real-world experience. No junior Air Force officer, even an engineer, was able to acquire such technical expertise in a two or three-year assignment.

My first clue to this reality was months earlier when I learned that my Vandenberg space launch training course would be just four weeks and not involve any simulator time. There was significant on-the-job training later at the Cape, but nothing approaching the detail of 16 weeks of Vandenberg missile training.

Eventually, I sat on console for two Atlas launches during my Cape assignment. Although I had several callouts over the communications network during the countdown, my primary responsibility was passing on status between my Air Force leadership sitting at another facility and the contractors in the blockhouse with me who directed the countdown procedure. Minor role or not, there is nothing quite as exciting as being on a launch day team.

For Air Force officers, console duty begins about five hours before the launch window opens. Although there is a specific time desired for launch, typically a launch window can be up to several hours. If a launch does not get off the ground within the window, then it is "scrubbed" for the day and another attempt is made the next day or soon after. This is because to reach a certain orbit, the earth's rotation must bring the launch site close to the overhead orbital insertion point. That window occurs only at a certain time each day. For some interplanetary launches those intersections might only happen a couple times a year, or even just once in over a hundred years!

On days I was to sit console, I would drive to a hangar located several miles away from the launch complex. There, with my headset and checklists in hand, I would board a bus which shuttled the 100 or so personnel working the launch to the blockhouse. When I first arrived at the Cape, launch duty personnel parked their cars near the pad. That practice was prohibited a month or so after I arrived, when a Delta II rocket carrying a GPS satellite blew up six seconds after launch, raining fiery debris and propellant down on the launch complex below it. Several cars and office trailers were destroyed in the process. So, no more parking on-site.

When the shuttle bus arrived at the complex, we all walked through the security gate and entered the above-ground blockhouse. This structure resembled a giant concrete igloo and was just 300 yards from the launch vehicle sitting on the pad. Once inside this fortress, the launch team was locked in behind a huge blast door reminiscent of the ones I knew from missiles. Like my old launch control center, the blockhouse had an escape tunnel. You could walk upright in this version. It was several hundred yards long, stretching underground and away from the launch pad. Its main purpose was for our evacuation in case of an on-pad, or over-the pad, explosion.

Once at our console seats, we would don our headsets and follow four and a half hours of countdown procedures. We checked off each step and call-out in a three-ring binder of almost 300 pages. Unlike missile control centers, there were video monitors throughout the blockhouse. From our seats we could view the Atlas II sitting on the pad, -298-degree liquid oxygen icing the sides and burn-off gases venting like smoke from on top.

In my training I'd learned that the Atlas II's skin was only the thickness of a dime. If it wasn't pressurized day to day, or before launch, with the volatile mix of kerosene-based fuel and liquid oxygen, it would collapse like crushed soda can. Despite its delicacy, this vehicle was capable of delivering a satellite to an orbit approximately 22,000 miles above the earth. At that location, the satellite orbits at the same rate as the earth's rotation making it appear to hover over a specific portion of the earth.

As the countdown continued, the tension in the blockhouse mounted. Many things can go wrong to either scrub a launch on the ground or cause it to fail to reach its intended orbit. Launches are delayed due to equipment failures, software issues, malfunctioning ground radars, space debris or the international space station passing overhead, even a single fishing boat drifting into the launch danger area.

Yet, the biggest driver of launch scrubs is weather. Florida has a well-earned reputation as the lightning capital of the world. A lightning strike can so debilitate a launch vehicle that there are stringent rules which forbid launching when certain cloud formations are near the launch pad or in the initial path of ascent. At many launch complexes, the highest and most visible structures on site are four lightning mitigation towers which protect the launch pad.

If the countdown avoided the above obstacles, anticipation soared with each milestone completed. At approximately two and a half hours before launch, the mobile service tower is rolled back away from the launch vehicle. This 20-story structure gives workers access to multi-levels of the launch vehicle during the weeks of on-pad processing. With 90 minutes left in the countdown, the pad is cleared and the launch vehicle is tanked with liquid hydrogen, liquid oxygen and fuel. Before the final minutes of countdown, there is a clock hold so all key system positions can be polled for their readiness to launch. I still get chills recalling the terse string of responses, "Go!," "Go!," "Go!"

When the launch vehicle lifted off in a mushroom of smoke and fire, I didn't need a video monitor to tell me what was happening right outside the blockhouse. The rumble vibrated within the control center and pounded on my chest. It was quite the adrenaline rush.

Sadly, for today's launch teams, that visceral immediacy is absent. There are newer launch vehicles at the Cape now and their control centers are a much safer, several miles away for the launch pad. Not that there aren't other launch innovations which still provide the thrill factor. New commercial launch providers like SpaceX are now flying back expended rocket stages which land back at Cape Canaveral to be re-used on future flights. United Launch Alliance, SpaceX and NASA are returning American astronauts to space, hopefully to create colonies on the Moon and later to travel on to Mars. My old launch complex is now leased to Jeff Bezos and his Blue Origin launch company, ensuring the Atlas IIs and Atlas IIIs won't be the last launch vehicles to soar from that location.

In the end, it all worked out well for me. I was so grateful I'd taken my father's advice and accepted the missile assignment offer. As he predicted, I did eventually move to a career field in which I was more interested and challenged. A quarter century later, I'm still working in space launch, but now as an Air Force civil servant.

I have returned to Grand Forks only once, just a couple years after ending my crew tour. The base is still there, but the missile wing was closed years ago, due to a nuclear treaty signed with Russia. In fact, of the six missile wings which were active when I began crew duty, only three still have strategic missiles. That's a good thing both for the country and for the world.

One of the launch control centers where I pulled alert, Oscar-Zero, is now part of the Ronald Reagan Minuteman Missile Historical Site run by the state of North Dakota. Tourists can drive out to the site near Cooperstown and take the elevator underground to walk through the capsule as it looked in the early 1990s. One day I'd like to visit. Maybe I'll bring my now-grown children or a grandchild to see where I served my country by spending 246 days and nights in the hole. It would be a nostalgic, yet surreal moment to stand beside my old chair among a group of tourists, maybe some of them Russian, while a guide describes that familiar operating equipment.

Looking back, I have a new appreciation for the unique experience of being a strategic missile warrior during the waning days of the Cold War. It wasn't always enjoyable, but like every challenging episode, there were moments to savor and hard lessons learned.

Two of my children were born in North Dakota and Beth became pregnant there with our third. Crew duty toughened me up and developed important personal traits which have served me well in the years since.

I've never enjoyed richer and closer military relationships than I did at Grand Forks. The decades since have not diminished those bonds. Even now, when I bump into an old missileer from those days, there's an immediate connection that I don't get with anyone else.

So, I wouldn't trade those four years in North Dakota for anything. Well, okay, there might be *some* things. Let's not get carried away. A missile crew assignment is like successful open-heart surgery. You are grateful you went through it, but you'd never want to do it again.

Yet, I'm proud of my service during those years. I believe that because I and my fellow missileers were on round-the-clock alert, the unthinkable was averted and our world was a safer place. In its own way, crew duty might be the most satisfying job I've ever had.

Index